A Voyage Through Time

By Margo Young

AuthorHouseTM
1663 Liberty Drive, Suite 200
Bloomington, IN 47403
www.authorhouse.com
Phone: 1-800-839-8640

FIRST EDITION

First published by AuthorHouse 7/30/2009

ISBN:978-1-4389-5874-3 (sc)
ISBN:978-1-4389-5970-2 (hc)

Printed in the United States of America
Bloomington, Indiana

This book is printed on acid-free paper.

Produced by
Writers Ink
Miami, Florida 33185

Writers Ink

Executive Editor
Robert Ratner

Design
Johann A. Marron Stefan for Studio Grafo

www.avoyagethroughtime.com
www.voyagethroughtime.com

authorHOUSE®

A Voyage Through Time

By Margo Young

Dedicated to my sister, Vera

Acknowledgments

I would like to thank my teacher and editor, Robert Ratner, who encouraged me, prodded me, and helped me write my memoirs. And I would like to thank Johann Marron Stefan, whose artistic design not only makes this book more beautiful but also allows me to tell my story through photographs and images.

In addition, I would like to thank my colleagues in my memoir writing seminar--Betsy, Maimie, Marian, Esther, Ruth, and Diane--whose patient advice has provided enduring support. And to my friends and family who have heard me say so many times that I was writing my life story, thanks for your love and for your faith in me. Here it is. Enjoy.

"Make voyages! Attempt them... there's nothing else."

- Tennessee Williams

Table of Contents

Author's Note
Forever Young

I am eighty-eight years old. My name is Margo Young, and I live in Bal Harbour, Florida. I get up every morning glad to be alive. I exercise, then spend my day doing as many things as I can. I recently cancelled a trip to South Africa. Instead, I decided to move to a new apartment with an even better view of the world: the city on one side, the ocean on the other. Three years ago, I was diagnosed with breast cancer. After the surgery, I told my doctor that I wanted the latest, best cancer-killing drugs available. I am now back to normal. I feel great. I feel more than great. I greet every day with hope and expectation. I start every evening by sipping a Scotch and watching the sunset, sometimes with family, sometimes with friends, sometimes by myself.

Someone asked me once why I did so much every day, why I traveled, why I packed so much into every day of my life? I didn't hesitate to answer. I know why. "I want to make sure that *I live deep and suck out all the marrow of life* before I get too old to enjoy it," I replied. You also might be wondering why I don't just settle down and marry again? I was married for forty-four years to the most wonderful man in the world, and it's my turn now. Not only do I like living, I like living alone.

Anyway, I'm not that easy to get along with. Don't get me wrong, I am sweet and sentimental and I have a generous heart, but I can also be demanding and downright grumpy if I don't get my way. I'm better off living alone. And you're better off not living with me.

But you can come visit any time. I am writing this book because I have something to say about how to live a fulfilling life. A lot of my story has to do with setting your mind on practical, achievable goals and persevering until you accomplish what you want to accomplish. I don't like taking no for an answer, but I also don't believe in sitting and sulking about what went wrong. Dysfunctional doesn't appear in my personal dictionary.

Being smart helps but anyone can learn to be smart. Staying healthy is paramount. And having money is essential. Absolutely essential. So this is my story, the story of how a plucky eighteen year old made her way out of pre-war Germany because she saw the shadow of the Nazis before she felt their presence and because she heard their goosesteps trampling her middle class comfort before their boots actually bore down on her. Although this is, in a sense, my diary, I was not and am not Anne Frank. Nor am I Robert Frost; my life is the opposite of *The Road Not Taken*. I lit out from Germany in 1938 and headed toward the promise of America as much for a sense of adventure as for the dark knowledge of the doom that was to come.

Even then, I wanted to live life fully and to beat life at its own game. I didn't want anyone crying over me because of my unrealized potential or because of the life I did not live. I didn't want anyone poring over the artifacts of my sad, snuffed-out life. Six million Jews died during the Holocaust. I was lucky. I did not. I always wanted to write my own story, but mine is not a story of escape or survival. My story is about success; it's about how to overcome adversity and succeed. It's about how to enjoy the opportunities life gives us. And while it may sound like a cliché, here it is, my story, *A Voyage Through Time, Forever Young* by Margo Young.

May you stay forever young. May we all stay forever young.

Bal Harbour, Florida

PART I

Chapter I
Coming to America

T he choppy waters outside New York Harbor split apart as the straight, insistent bow of the *R.M.S. Britannic* moves determinedly toward shore.

The sea folds back far below me in a foamy, hard sloshing wake along the ship's dark sides. I look out from one of the highest decks but have trouble seeing what is below; still, I can hear the mew of the gulls, the rush of the wind, and the sounds of emotion all around. I pull away from the others for a moment to a place all alone.

My grip clenches tighter on the salty railing of the Cunard liner's top deck. I feel a peculiar connection with her; she has, after all, carried me across the ocean. I am a young émigré of eighteen; it is October 23, 1938; I want to know exactly what I am seeing, and I want to know everything I am feeling. Margot Schragenheim from Hamburg, Germany always likes to know exactly what is going on around her.

My hair snaps in the wind like the ship's flags; I pull a scarf over my head, tuck in the flyaway strands, and cinch the scarf under my chin. I look straight ahead at the water. When a family leaves the railing to go down below, I take their place on the starboard side of the ship. Everyone anxiously moves closer and closer to where they will exit to meet their loved ones.

We turn slowly, edging to the right, past the base of Long Island, toward the Hudson River basin. I have time to watch. I am already packed. In the fresh breeze of a glorious autumn day, I look around me, drawing everything in.

The wind whips the blue-green sea into small whitecaps. Slowly, we move into the more protected harbor waters and make several small, subtle turns in the channel as we head toward the still unseen city. The powerful ship moves forward and the world around me seems to rotate and change as the ocean liner shifts direction into the huge port. Three black-banded funnels painted classic "Cunard Red," a hot, reddish-orange really, rise in the cobalt-colored sky, and my eyes strain to see the shimmering, vibrating towers set against the cool blue above me.

I am glad to be holding the railing. I say a silent prayer for my parents and sister, who I wish were with me. It has been quite a crossing but I am safe, and I am almost to my new home now.

The tugboats join us. The ship makes another slow turn in the channel, and I catch my breath. There, ahead to the right, on a small island almost incapable of sustaining her resplendent majesty, is the sight I have heard about--and dreamed of--for so long. Proof of my passage. Proof of my transition into adulthood. Proof I have made it and am alive. There in front of me is the Statue of Liberty.

I knew her well. I had seen pictures of this woman, welcoming the tired, the poor, and the tempest-tossed. This verdigris-burnished statue held out the hope of a new beginning. But to finally see the Lady of the Harbor, to see her in front of me, with her spiked nimbus and her arm lifted, her gilded beacon flaming for freedom, I am overcome.

The *R. M. S. Britannic* and the Manhattan skyline

I nod silently to the Mother of Exiles and ready myself to take my place among the new immigrants coming to America.

The tugboats pilot the 27,000-ton ship into the harbor, and fireboats spray water in high rainbow arcs. Manhattan, with its jagged skyline of skyscrapers, spreads out in front of me. The tugs nudge and snuggle us close to the pier.

People are weeping. People are laughing. Some are shouting. Many are jumping up and down and clapping their hands like little children.

As we get closer, everyone on the pier begins to scream, and I hear taxis honking their horns in response to the ship's blaring arrival. I stand on deck, all alone, wondering what the future might have in store for me. I think about the tumultuous three years that have led me to this New World. I've left behind my entire family, and I have a long way to go to prove I've made the right decision. We slip decorously past The Lady with the Lamp and I square my shoulders and calm myself: *Okay, Margot,* I say to myself, *Okay, you wanted this, and now it's yours. It's time to get going. Time's a wasting. It's showtime!*

Chapter II

We Don't Want Jews Here

I'd boarded the *R.M.S. Britannic* seven days earlier in South Southampton, England, October 17, 1938. I'd turned eighteen just two months before.

In 1935, when I was only fifteen, despite the chaos churning around me our lives had not yet drastically changed. But I had read Hitler's book, *Mein Kampf*, and it certainly seemed to me Jews in Nazi Germany were doomed. It was clear that Hitler wanted to exterminate all the Jews of Germany.

The so-called "Nuremberg Laws" limiting the civil rights of Jews had passed that year, and we were all aware of the dire implications. Instead of pursuing a degree in law, I quit school. I saw no future in an academic career. Instead, I decided to become a secretary, a faster, more direct route to independence. It would allow me to support myself when the time came for me to emigrate.

My involvement in Jewish youth organizations also made me especially aware of the ominous future we faced. I had discussed emigration with my parents and relatives, but nobody took the ideas of a fifteen-year old seriously.

I knew that my mother's father, Grosspapa Böninger, had a sister living in the United States. My hope was that she would sponsor my immigration. She had fallen in love with a man the family did not approve of, a house painter with a limited education and a very limited income. Her upper middle class family was aghast when she insisted on marrying him.

Before 1924, it had been possible to immigrate to the United States without a sponsor and without meeting stringent requirements, so it was suggested to the newlyweds that they immigrate to America. The family bought them passage and gave them money and off they went. Grosspapa was the only one of the brothers who had stayed in touch with them. He loved his only sister very much, and they kept up a steady correspondence. I asked Grosspapa for their address so that I could write and ask for their help obtaining the necessary papers to come to America.

"Forget about them," Grosspapa said. "The Meyers are very poor people who just eke out a living from their house painting."

"But I could try," I insisted.

"No use at all. It would only embarrass them," was his answer.

I forced myself to forget about Grosspapa's sister, but I came up with another idea of how I might obtain a so-called "affidavit"--the necessary document to immigrate to the United States.

I went to the main office of the Hamburg Telephone Company. I thought that New York, the largest city in the U.S.A, might be a good place to start. I wanted to find any distant relatives who might send me the necessary immigration papers. I did not find any Schragenheims or Böningers, but I did find a number of Enochs, my paternal grandmother's maiden name, and I found even more Wagners, which was the maiden name of my maternal grandmother. It was not a particularly Jewish name, but a very common German one.

I had learned enough English to write a decent letter, and I wrote to all the people I found in the phone book. I told them who I was and how I thought we might be related. I told them how I had found their names and addresses and that I desperately needed to find a sponsor.

I promised never to become a burden. "I am independent. I can stand on my own feet," I said. I laid out my qualifications: I could take care of children. I could clean, wash, and iron. I sewed, cooked, and baked. My mother had made sure that we learned everything a future wife and homemaker should know. I hoped it would be enough to land me a sponsor.

After all my hard work, I did not receive one single reply. It was very disappointing, but it merely meant that I had to find another way to get to America.

We were in the latter part of 1937 by this time, and life for Jews in Germany had deteriorated noticeably. No longer could we attend the theater or concerts or the opera. Jewish doctors and lawyers could no longer practice their professions, and my father had to sell his business. I vividly remember being in a vegetarian restaurant where my friends and I frequently met for lunch. After ordering, I looked up and saw a large sign with the words,

JUDEN SIND HIER NICHT ERWUENSCHT
(WE DON'T WANT JEWS HERE)

Silently, I motioned to my friend to look up, and without a further word we got up and walked slowly out of the restaurant.

That evening, I went to see Grosspapa, and I told him what had happened and begged him to give me the address of his sister, Bertha Meyer, in Irvington, New Jersey.

He relented. I wrote to her immediately, telling her who I was, that I hoped she and her husband could send me the necessary affidavit, and that I would be forever grateful to her. I promised to work hard, to be an asset to the family, and to never ever become a financial burden to her and her family.

Bertha and her husband wrote back that they would sponsor me and that I should send them the required documents. They would send me the affidavit with the help of the Council of Jewish Women.

I was ecstatic. I had succeeded. I sometimes look back and wonder where I got all that gumption. Despite my family's misgivings, I

Margot at age 18

was determined to go. And I was lucky to have the chance.

Only a limited number of people from each country was allowed to immigrate to the United States each year. When I applied, it was still fairly easy to obtain a quota number as a German citizen. A few months later, however, in March of 1938, the German government annexed Austria. Now we were not only afraid of what would happen to Jews in Nazi Germany, we were also afraid that Hitler would annex other countries and that war would break out and trap us in Germany without escape. In 1933, some 523,000 Jews lived in Germany, 17,000 of whom lived in my hometown of Hamburg. The quota quickly filled up as more and more Jews applied to go to America. Some people who had perfect affidavits could no longer get permission to leave Germany.

By September of 1939, however, 282,000 Jews had found ways to get out of Germany. Some were lucky and found refuge in other countries, but, unfortunately, many could not find a way to get out of Germany and later perished in the concentration camps.

Sometime in August of 1938, around the time of my 18th birthday, I received the anxiously awaited notification from the American Consulate in Hamburg. My required interview and physical examination were scheduled for September. To my chagrin, my appointment turned out to be on the first day of Rosh Hashanah. While I saw this as a good omen, I was still more than a little worried about my papers being in order and about actually obtaining this coveted entry visa into the United States.

I clearly remember walking from our apartment to the consulate, about 45 to 50 minutes away. Although I usually had no compunction about riding on the holidays, my Orthodox background reminded me it was a sin to ride on the Jewish New Year, and I had the worrisome feeling that if I didn't walk I might somehow jeopardize my entry visa. I was hoping that G-d was looking out for me.

Everything went well at the interview and physical examination and in a few days I received notification from the consulate that my entry visa to the United States had been approved. Now I had to visit the consulate again, only this time on Yom Kippur, the holiest day of the Jewish year, the Day of Atonement. Again, I made the 50-minute walk. When I arrived out of breath from the walk and from anticipation, the Consul himself handed me the magnificent document I had sought for so long as if it were the Holy Grail. It bore a red seal with the words, *United States of America.* The blue ribbon that stretched diagonally across the parchment seemed to glow. I finally held in my hands my visa to America and to my future.

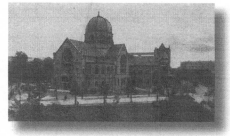

I left the consulate and headed to the big *Bornplatz* Synagogue where my grandparents and other relatives worshipped. I went upstairs to the seat where my grandmother Schragenheim sat and showed The Bornplatz Synagogue

her the visa. She kissed me and blessed me with tears in her eyes.

I could *not* go downstairs where the men were worshiping, but I quietly made the rounds to all my aunts, other relatives, and friends. There were kisses and whispers of "Mazel Tov," everyone careful not to disturb the service. Everybody was happy for me, but they were also worried about their own futures. I never saw any of them again after I left Germany.

From the *Bornplatz* Synagogue, I went to our temple at the *Oberstrasse*, where my father, my mother, and my younger sister, Vera, and our friends were waiting for me at the services. I didn't

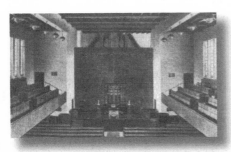

even wait until I got to their seats. I waved the visa at them the moment I entered the upstairs portion of the temple where they were sitting.

My Daddy looked up from his seat downstairs and when he saw me waving the visa, he raised his hand in salute and

Inside the *Oberstrasse* Temple

threw me a kiss. If Rabbi Italiener was disturbed by this undignified interruption of the service, he showed absolutely no sign of it.

Margot's passport stamped "J" for Jew, 1938

Chapter III
The Unknown Future

That evening, we sat around the dining room table to break the fast and began discussing the details of my emigration in earnest. With the papers finally in front of us, my eventual departure became a reality. They say the young are self-centered, well, I plead guilty. I was so emboldened to be going--so excited and thrilled to finally be escaping Germany--that I don't think I realized how hard it must have been for my parents to accept the fact that their firstborn was leaving. And I was leaving them behind. I was so happy to be going that I refused to see anything wrong with it. My parents were careful to hide their fears and to keep their doubts to themselves. What a difference that made. I have subsequently discovered this same philosophy. You must wholeheartedly embrace a challenge if you expect to succeed at it.

I told Mutti, my mother, and Daddy that I wanted to leave as quickly as possible and that I would make all the necessary arrangements myself. I needed an exit permit from the German authorities, and there were specific procedures and regulations about the inspection of the luggage I wanted to take along; of course, I also had to book passage. I wanted to take a ship out of England because my dearest girlfriend, Lore Baral, had left for London some six months earlier and I wanted to see her again.

Mutti and Daddy were re-
signed to this trip by now, and
they agreed to pay for my passage and give me the 500 marks
I was permitted to take out of
the country. That amounted to
$125.00. We knew it was not
very much, even in 1938, for a
young girl to start life in a new
country, but I told them that I
would manage. Looking back, I
am amazed at how mature and
self confident I was at the age
of eighteen, and, after all, I did
manage to take care of all the arrangements and paperwork on
my own without any problems.

Lore Baral

That same evening, I solemn-
ly begged Mutti and Daddy to
let me take my 14-year-old sister, Vera, with me. Even though
I knew that getting her papers
would postpone my departure,
I was willing to wait if it meant
that I could take her with me. I
think in the back of my mind I
was half-afraid that my family
would lose their nerve to leave
Germany. It was asking an awful lot for them to leave everybody and everything behind. I
knew in my soul that we had to

Vera at age 14

get away from Hitler, and I wanted Vera safe with me in America. Most of all, I also knew if I had Vera, my parents would follow.

I promised my parents that I would take good care of my little sister, but Mutti and Daddy refused to let Vera come with me. They felt that I was much too young to take on the responsibility of my sister, and I also think that they could not bear the thought of losing both daughters at the same time. I promised to get immigration papers for them very quickly so that our entire family could be reunited in America.

The next day, I went to the Cunard Line office and booked passage on the *R.M.S. Britannic*, which was sailing out of Southampton, England on October 17th and was scheduled to arrive in New York on October 23rd. The passage included a train trip from Hamburg to the Hook of Holland. After that, I would share a two-bed cabin on a ferry across the English Channel to Harwich, England, then board a train to London. In London, I would stay in a hotel for three nights and then take another train from London to Southampton to board the ship.

All this preparation and excitement--a trip of this magnitude--the start of a new life for me--was mind-boggling. I was almost delirious with excitement, and while I was sad to leave my family I did not have the time to dwell on it. I could not afford to think sad thoughts. I simply had to convince myself that I could earn a living and would be able to send papers for Mutti, Daddy, and Vera to join me soon.

Then just as I was preparing to go, German troops invaded Czechoslovakia. It was right after the Munich Pact, when Neville Chamberlain, the British prime minister, met with Adolf Hitler in an attempt to assure peace in Europe. Very few people, however, believed that peace would prevail. We knew Hitler was hungry for territory and power. When the troops marched into the Sudetenland in September of 1938, most of my friends felt that Hitler would not stop, that he would want to go further, and that war was imminent. I remember standing with my friends on *Eppendorfer Baum* discussing the situation. I should leave for England immediately and await my passage there, I thought. But Mutti and Daddy felt that I should arrange my departure in an orderly manner. I took their advice and eventually left as scheduled on October 13th.

Before leaving, however, I had to go to the office where exit visas were issued. It was a frightening experience with lots of uniformed SA and SS officers milling about. My passport, which I already had, was stamped with a big red "J" for "JUDE" (Jew), but things went as planned, and my exit visa was granted.

The last step was to have my steamer trunk transported to the so-called "free port" where its contents would be examined. The Cunard Line would take it from there, shipping it to England. Once the trunk arrived at the free port, I had to go down there with a list of its contents and a key to open it for inspection.

The people were actually very nice and, as it turned out, after looking at the list of contents, they didn't even make me open the trunk. I guess I could have smuggled out money, diamonds, and all kinds of valuables, but who would take that chance? The only thing I hid was a silver breadbasket Grossmutti gave me to remind me of her and of her beautiful silver which she so much had wanted me to have. Grossvati's "goodbye" present was a *Saks* prayer book containing the most important and useful prayers and blessings, which he inscribed with a warm and beautiful dedication. I still use this prayer book and I will treasure it to the end of my days.

Grossmutti's silver breadbasket

There were many beautiful presents from relatives and friends. I remember vividly Grosspapa's gift. It was an ultra-chic leather handbag that had a storage space for a matching compact and umbrella on the bottom, quite a novelty at that time! Unfortunately, it has vanished, but the sweet memory of how he had tried so hard to give his granddaughter something so stylish and so different stays with me.

On the 13th of October, just seven weeks after my 18th birthday, Mutti, Daddy, and Vera took me to the train at the *Hauptbahnhof* (the central railroad station) where we said a very tearful goodbye. I remember looking at their faces, etching them into my memory, fearing for them, praying this was not the last time I would see them or hold them close.

The colors of the October leaves were vibrant and the sun shone brilliantly on the rivers and lakes that we passed along the way. As the train continued toward the west and we approached the Rhine River, the landscape changed.

In the distance, we saw old castles on the hilltops, and vineyards bordered the roadbed. The train roared ahead toward the city of Aachen and the Dutch border. I was blithely indifferent to the German and Dutch border police. I knew that my papers were in good order: why should I worry? This was an adventure. I was looking forward to crossing the Channel, seeing London for the first time, and meeting my girlfriend, Lore Baral. And I was even more excited about crossing the ocean, arriving in New York, and starting life again all on my very own. I could not imagine the danger crossing these same borders would entail just a short time later.

I started talking to a young woman riding near me. It turned out that we were both taking the same ferry across the English Channel, and after chatting for a while we decided, if we could, to share the same cabin on the ferry. This turned out to be an unfortunate decision on my part because the poor girl became horribly seasick the minute we got in the cabin, and she stayed sick all the way to the English port of Harwich.

I don't remember it being that bad. I wasn't sick, but then again I never got seasick. I had spent so much of my leisure time on the water in small canoes and sailboats that I suppose my system was used to it. But the English Channel is known for rough waters, and it was making my cabin mate's life miserable. As for me, I wasn't very happy in a cabin that reeked from seasickness, so at four in the morning I got dressed and went up on deck.

The water may have been rough but the stars were shining, and as it wasn't too cold yet, the wind and the fresh sea air were a decided improvement. Just as we were approaching the English coast, the Sun rose like a huge fireball behind us. It gilded the coastline ahead, washed it in golden light, as if to tell me that my life to come would be a treasure for the taking.

A Cunard Line representative met the ferry and put us on the proper train to London. To this day, I have not forgotten the magnificent, lush green that was all around us; England's landscapes took my breath away. Germany's countryside was certainly beautiful, but nothing could compare to my first impressions of England. The fields and forests and meadows were the stuff of sonnets and legends come alive.

My girlfriend, Lore, met me at the railroad station. We hugged and kissed for a long time, simply glad to see each other again. It had been months since she'd left Hamburg. We took a taxi to the small hotel where the Cunard Line had booked a room for me. I don't remember much about the place except that I was given an absolutely enormous room key. It's funny what the mind remembers, but never in my 18 years had I seen a key that was so big. In this mythic adventure of mine, it too became a symbol: I knew I would soon unlock the whole wide world.

Lore told me she was living with an Indian man. She did not introduce him to me, but she didn't seem ashamed of him either. I think she just wanted to spend our time alone, have some private girl-to-girl time together. And so did I.

I was astonished by the change Lore had undergone since I'd last seen her in Hamburg. She had wanted to be an Orthodox Jew, and now she was living with a man of a different faith to whom she was not married!

She explained to me that it had been hard living with her aunt and uncle. She liked them and she liked her cousins, but she did not like the restrictions they placed on her. She had met the Indian, she was fond of him, and since she was not self-supporting she had moved in with him. How could I criticize her? We were young and open to new experiences and adventures. I was just happy to see her again.

Lore took me sightseeing, and I was very impressed with London: this historic, beautiful city with its green parks, its churches, its bridges, its beautiful hotels around Hyde Park, and, of course, with Buckingham Palace. The next day, I would board the ship.

Lore picked me up at the hotel and after having breakfast together she took me to the station where I caught the train to Southampton and the *R.M.S. Britannic* for my crossing to the United States.

It was the last time I saw my friend Lore. For a while after I was in America we wrote back and forth. Then her letters suddenly stopped. I couldn't imagine why she would stop writing. Had I said something wrong? Worried, I wrote to her cousin in London whose address she had given me and asked what had happened to Lore. Why wasn't she answering my letters?

His reply made me sad. Her parents and younger brother who were all Polish citizens were forced to leave Germany, and since they had no immigration papers to any other country they went back to Lodz in Poland, their original hometown.

When Lore did not hear from them after they had been in Poland for a while, she decided to go look for them. That was all her cousin knew at that time. We stayed in touch, and shortly after the war I learned that when the Germans occupied Poland all four of the Baral family were sent to a concentration camp, where they died.

The *R.M.S. Britannic* was a beautiful ocean liner similar to the ones we occasionally visited when they were docked in the Hamburg Harbor. I had a small outside cabin for myself, and I became swept up in the enthusiasm aboard the ship; it turns out, there were quite a number of young Jews from Germany and Austria making the same journey I was. The very first evening, we formed a congenial group and had a marvelous time together. We danced and walked and talked on deck until the wee hours of the night. The next day, we sat on deck and told each other stories and sang our familiar songs. Short shipboard romances blossomed. We laughed a lot. Even though we had left our loved ones behind and the future was so uncertain, we were young and full of anticipation. I believe we were genuinely optimistic; after all, we'd managed to escape and we were heading toward a new world filled with possibilities.

But after two days of easy passage, the ocean became brutal. The big liner began to shake and roll and sway. The tables in the dining room had tray-like, curved wooden edges, so that the dishes and silverware would not slide off. It was a good thing. That night, we needed them.

After dinner, when I was dancing and enjoying the company of one of the young men, I noticed that we were dancing on only one side of the dance floor. I wondered why. After a few minutes, I asked him.

"If you would look the other way," he answered, "you would know." Sure enough, I looked and saw that the whole room, including the dance floor, was tilting at a very steep angle.

The next morning, only a few people came to breakfast. The hallways carried the foul smell of seasickness, and the ship continued shaking and vibrating as if it too was still ill. There were a few rugged people, myself included, in the dining room.

Everybody there had a recommendation about what to eat in order to avoid seasickness: pickled herring and pumpernickel was one possibility. A few of us really didn't care and we ate our usual breakfast. Then I went up on deck for fresh air. It was fresh all right! The wind was howling, and the waves were so high that they looked like mountains with snowcaps on them.

A British girl and I were the only two brave ones up there enjoying the spectacular view. We found a protected spot with two deck chairs, asked the deck steward for blankets, and sat back in the chaises to enjoy the "brisk" ocean air. Our daffy pleasure didn't last too long before an officer came to chase us inside. He looked astonished to find us where we were, and he told us the ocean was getting rougher and rougher and the waves would soon reach the deck. "Please, please, hurry inside," he said. "I do not want you fine ladies to be washed overboard."

After a day or two, the ocean finally calmed down. Most everybody came out of their cabins still looking a little queasy, but, young as we were, we all perked up quickly and continued having a jolly time throughout the rest of the crossing.

There was, of course, great commotion after the ship was safely docked at its pier on 12th Avenue on the Westside of New York City. Relatives and friends came to meet passengers, and everyone seemed to be shouting and crying and hugging and kissing all at the same time.

Charles Meyer and his son, Charlie, said they would pick me up, but although I had a picture of them I really did not know what they looked like. Many of the passengers had left the ship by now, but nobody had called my name yet.

A friendly woman, a staff member or someone from immigration, asked me whether anybody would be meeting me. I told her who they were and she promised to call their names over the loudspeaker system and to look for them.

"Oh, well," I said to myself, "if they don't come, I'll just ask somebody for the name of a decent hotel, get a taxi, and call them from there."

I had found in London that I spoke enough English to get by, so I was not too worried, but while I was making these contingency plans in my head the Meyers appeared, glad to have finally found me.

Charles Meyer was in his fifties. He was a pleasant man of medium height and build, with reddish hair and a fair complexion. He gave me a warm hug and welcomed me to America. His son, Charlie, was very good-looking with dark, wavy hair and big, soft brown eyes. In his late twenties, he was taller than his father and more solidly built. Both were friendly and kind and tried their best to make me feel comfortable.

After I spoke a few words, Charlie said to his father, "Listen to her. She even speaks English. How wonderful." They must have been wondering what they were going to do with a young immigrant who spoke only German. We found my steamer trunk and muscled it into their old car and off we went through the huge Holland tunnel underneath the Hudson River toward New Jersey and my unknown future.

Chapter IV
My Story Begins,
The Schragenheims

My paternal grandparents--Elias and Claire Schragenheim--lived in a large apartment on the fourth floor on *Gneisenaustrasse*, in a section of Hamburg called Hoheluft (high air) that was not too far from our home.

It was an elegant, old apartment, and I recall it well. My earliest memories are from before Vera and I were old enough for school, when we spent every other weekend with our grandparents. While Vera was not as keen about these regular visits as I was, I looked forward to them very much.

On Friday mornings, Mutti would help us pick out our dresses to wear. Our mother was a fashion designer, and all our clothes were handmade and lovely. We dressed like twins in matching outfits she'd made for us. She would deliver us to our grandparents' home and return later with my father for dinner. We spent the day playing and helping Grossmutti in the kitchen prepare the Shabbat dinner.

They had a bright, cheery living room that was decorated tastefully by my grandmother. There she entertained my mother and my aunts and her lady friends. And, of course, my sister and I played there, too. She had an antique sewing table in one corner that fascinated me. It was made of light mahogany and had delicate curved legs and drawers and a fairy tale quality to it. It was filled with Grossmutti's spools of yarn, needles, scissors, ribbons, and whatever handiwork project she was working on.

On the other hand, Gross-vati enjoyed his library filled with shelves of leather-covered books. For me as a child, it was a dark, foreboding place, but as I got older I realized the books and Oriental rugs actually made it cozy. This was his retreat and

Elias Schragenheim in his library

he sat there to read or work at his desk, and he would host other men in there after dinner for a cognac and, if it wasn't Friday night (smoking was not allowed on the Shabbat), to smoke a cigar.

The bedroom, which Vera and I shared when we came to visit, still had the toys that had belonged to our father and his brother, Bruno.

The apartment also included a very large kitchen and maids' quarters. Since it was a strictly kosher household, there were two tables, two sinks, and two stoves, one for *fleischig* (meat) and one for *milchig* (dairy). When I was about six years old, I committed the unpardonable sin of putting a milchig spoon on the fleischig table. I was scolded severely and I remember crying and being ashamed of myself because they would have to tell Grossvati what I'd done. They would also have to clean everything thoroughly and say a blessing.

Because we spent many Sabbath evenings there having wonderful Friday night dinners, I remember the dining room's every detail. It was an ornate room with light mahogany furniture. There was a very long dining table that when extended could seat 40 to 50 people. It was a tricky piece of furniture and it intrigued me. When pulled apart, built-in leaves would appear, and underneath each leaf additional table legs dropped down for support. It fascinated me so that I made sure I was always close by when anyone began to open that table.

On one wall of the dining room there was a huge cabinet, which rose almost to the ceiling. It contained my grandmother's various sets of Hutschenreuther and Rosenthal china, as well as her sterling silver platters, breadbaskets, and other serving dishes. There were shelves with sparkling crystal glasses and goblets. I especially loved the ones for cordials, delicate and thinner than rose petals.

Partitioned drawers opened showing perfectly organized sets of gleaming sterling flatware: full services with every kind and size of knife, fork, and spoon used in formal dining. There were all the beautiful serving pieces: ladles and meat forks and carving knives and captivating tiny trident spears for pickles and condiments. One day, when I was helping my grandmother set the table, she opened all the doors and drawers of the cabinet and said, "Look, my darling girl, look at all these beautiful things. One day, all of this will be yours."

But it was not to be. When I left for the United States in October of 1938, I smuggled out the one silver breadbasket she had given me by wrapping it in clothing and hiding it in my trunk. In 1939, Hitler decreed that Jews could no longer possess valuables, and everything was turned over to the authorities. My silver breadbasket is all that remains of Grossmutti's lovely things.

Friday nights were always very festive; the table was dressed in starched white damask and all the wonderful silver adorned each place setting. Two tall silver candlesticks with white candles stood in the center of the table.

Shortly before sundown, Grossmutti would say to me, "Now stand next to me while I light the candles. I want you to learn the blessing because one day you will light Shabbat candles, too." She would lift her hands and say the Hebrew prayers.

Barukh atah Adonai, Eloheinu, melekh ha'olam

Blessed are you, Lord, our God, sovereign of the universe

asher kidishanu b'mitz'votav v'tzivanu

Who has sanctified us with His commandments and commanded us

l'had'lik neir shel Shabbat.

to light the lights of Shabbat.

Then she would have us stand in front of her. I can remember her placing her gentle hands on each of our heads to bless us while she softly chanted: *Yevarech Adonai* ("May G-d Bless You").

As soon as the men came home from Friday night services, we would sit down for dinner. Sometimes there were extra guests, but usually it was just our parents, and our father's younger brother, Bruno, and his wife, Irma. Aunt Irma would always ask, "Margo, did you help your grandmother cook today?"

Grossvati would lift the silver cup and chant the blessings for the wine and for the freshly baked *challah*, which grandmother kept covered with an embroidered satin cover.

The meal was served by two maids who wore long-sleeved, gray uniforms with little white starched aprons and matching caps on their heads. Grandmother was very particular and everything had to be served correctly. She was an excellent cook and baker, and despite having help she cooked everything herself. At the end of the meal, Grossvati would never fail to say to her, "Claire, my darling, your meal was once again exceptional tonight."

Grossvati Schragenheim was born in 1870 in Verden-an-der Aller, a small German town in the province of Hanover, one of the youngest among thirteen children. Unfortunately, I only met two of his siblings: a brother who lived in Bremen and a sister who lived in Breslau. When my great aunt came to Hamburg, she would take me to a favorite coffee house where we enjoyed the most delicious cakes I ever tasted. She died in India where she lived with her son after fleeing Hitler's Germany.

Grossvati was a short, slim man with a white Vandyke beard and bushy, dark eyebrows. He was an independent certified public accountant, always impeccably dressed in custom-made suits, long sleeved shirts with cufflinks, and well-knotted silk ties. He was a man of habit. Every morning, he bathed in ice-cold water in his huge bathtub; he was convinced it helped both his circulation and his constitution.

Elias Schragenheim

He was a stern man, who took things seriously and rarely smiled except when he played with us, the grandchildren. After the Friday night dinners, he would take Vera and me on his lap and sing *Zemiros* songs to us. In his role of grandfather, he smiled happily and sang energetically, telling us silly stories and making rabbits out of the dinner napkins. We giggled and tugged on his beard.

He assumed that his children were Orthodox and observant and that his grandchildren would be brought up in the same manner. However, my father had become more liberal, and unbeknownst to Grossvati, instead of walking over to his parents' Friday night dinners he surreptitiously drove my mother over in our car. Daddy would hide the car around the corner so he would not offend his parents and stir up trouble. One Friday night, Grossvati wanted to walk us home. It was a beautiful spring evening and he felt a nice walk would be a good idea after a heavy meal. So we all took a walk with him to our house about half an hour away; the next morning, Daddy had to go back to pick up his car.

When Hitler came to power, we could no longer employ gentile maids to turn lights on and off on the Sabbath, a task which Orthodox Jews were forbidden to do. So Grossvati, who liked gadgets, installed a Shabbat timer, an invention he took great pride and pleasure in. On Friday night it worked like magic, except for one minor problem: all the lights turned off while we were still in the hallway getting dressed to leave.

But Grossvati was delighted that his device actually worked. "Now isn't that great" he said. "This invention really does work!"

"Yes," I remember Daddy answered him laughing, "but it would work even better if we could find our coats and hats."

My grandmother Claire Schragenheim's maiden name was Enoch and she was born in the city of Hanover, which was not far from Verden. She had three or four brothers, but only one was alive during my childhood. I knew her three sisters, however, my aunts Anna, Martha, and Laura.

My grandmother was the most beautiful of all her sisters. I don't have a picture of her as a young woman, but the picture I do have still shows lovely features. She had long, black hair, and I remember her sitting at her dressing table, a hairdresser brushing her hair, stroke after stroke. She wore her lovely dark hair severely pulled back from her forehead and wound into a chignon at the back of her head.

Claire Schragenheim

Grossmutti was always beautifully outfitted. One of Hamburg's best dressmakers made her pure silk dresses in wonderful prints. She owned a few fur coats and the one I liked best was made of lustrous, black fur, trimmed with a beige collar and cuffs.

I don't know how my grandparents met. I suppose like most Jewish marriages of that time it was arranged by either a *chadchen* (a marriage broker), a relative, or a friend of the family. Both Claire and Elias had come from liberal Jewish homes, but they both became Orthodox before their marriage. I have no idea about my grandfather's turn to Orthodoxy, but Grossmutti had once been in love with an Orthodox rabbi's son, and she became Orthodox because of him; maybe Grandfather became Orthodox because she was?

My grandparents, particularly my grandmother, had a great influence on me. They instilled in me certain formative values: a love for religion and its traditions and proper speech and manners were especially important to them. They set high standards. My grandmother encouraged in me an appreciation of music and the arts, and she took me to concerts and recitals. She fostered in me a love for elegant dining and refined surroundings and a deep appreciation of paintings, silver, and china, of lovely objects that can add such grace and polish to life.

The advice and suggestions from grandparents like mine, when presented with love, diplomacy, and understanding, are powerful models for young minds. I've always considered myself tremendously fortunate to have grown up with such loving and caring grandparents.

My grandfather, Elias Schragenheim, died of a heart attack in 1938, the year I escaped from Germany. My grandmother, Claire, died of cancer a year later in 1939.

Chapter V
The Böningers

My mother's parents, the Böningers, were different from the Schragenheims. While they were Orthodox Jews, they were much more informal and not as rigid as my father's family. My grandfather, Moses Böninger, who was called "Moritz," was from Cologne and he had the temperament and "joie de vivre" so typical of people from the Rhine region of Germany.

Grosspapa's family owned a chain of men's clothing stores in Cologne, and they sent him to Hamburg when he was twenty to learn how to become a successful businessman. He married my grandmother, Mery Wagner, when he was only twenty-three years old. She was nine or ten years older than my grandfather, but she was very beautiful and charming.

I have no idea why she had remained unmarried until then. She was originally from Altona, a twin city of Ham-

Moses Böninger

burg, and had a brother, Moritz Wagner, as well as two sisters, Hannah and Adele.

My grandmother, Mery, died at sixty of a heart attack. I was only six, so I have few memories of her, but I do recall the Friday night dinners at the Böningers. I was brought over to their house Friday morning because Grossmama wanted to spend extra time with her first grandchild.

She would put me in a chair in the kitchen while she prepared the Friday evening and Shabbat meals. I still see her donning a big, black apron and frying flounders on the stove. She heated oil in huge frying pans, and one by one she would very gently begin placing the flounders in the hot oil so that they would not break apart. "You see, my child," she would say, "you always know when a flounder is fresh. When you drop it into the hot fat and the tail of the flounder lifts up, then you are sure that the flounder is fresh."

"Wenn der Schwantz in die Hoehe geht is der Fisch frisch."

I was sure she was trying to teach me something.

Since we lived in Hamburg, which is a port city on the River Elbe and not far from the North Sea, we always got the best and freshest fish. There was a huge fish market in nearby Altona, and there was an abundance of other fish besides the tasty flounder. There was cod, turbot, haddock, shrimp, and lobster. There was also fresh water fish: salmon from the River Rhine, eels from the Weichsel, trout

Mery Böninger

from the mountain brooks, and carp from the neighboring lakes.

The fried flounders Grossmama prepared were served cold with home-made potato salad and were accompanied by cold coffee for the Sabbath midday meal when everyone returned from services at the synagogue.

My grandparents Böninger lived on *Bornstrasse*, just a short walk from *Bornplatz*, where the main synagogue of Hamburg was located, a magnificent building with a round cupola and a beautifully adorned sanctum. While in all Orthodox synagogues men and women sit separately, the *Bornplatz* had a mixed choir of boys and girls on the upper level of the synagogue, a little higher than the women's section. When I was a little girl, I attended services every Sabbath. The men still wore top hats and morning coats and striped trousers. They wore gray or gray and black striped ties, adorned with pearl or diamond stickpins.

The Böningers' apartment was spacious, like that of the Schragenheims, but it was cozier and not quite as elegant. There was a large dining room, a living room, and a library. Along the hallway were bedrooms, and all the way at the end of the kitchen there was a maid's bedroom. The Böningers had only one maid, who did most of the housework, and she helped in the kitchen and served at mealtimes. They had extra help for the heavy housework and a laundress who came in once a week.

The meals at the Böningers were not as formal as those at the Schragenheims and because of this they were much more fun. There was usually a huge roast on the table, which Grosspapa carved himself, passing slices to our plates. My mother's only brother, Uncle Martin,

The Böningers with their three children, Bianka, Selma, and Martin

who was three years younger than she, was still unmarried in those years and he lived at home. My mother's sister, Bianka, who was three years older than she, had married when I was a little girl. She and her very handsome husband, Uncle Siegfried, would usually visit during these Friday dinners.

Passover Seders were divided between the two families. The first Seder was at the Schragenheims, and the second one was at the Böningers. Both Seders were very, very long and hardly a word was left out from the *Hagadah*. Each presiding grandfather added his own lengthy explanations in German, and though it dragged on the grandfathers tried their best to make things as interesting as possible for the children. In the end, they did a pretty good job. What I liked best were the songs during the Seder service, especially the ones at the end of the ceremony. Each family sang them a little differently, sometimes to completely different tunes.

I remember one of my first Seders at the Böningers when I was five or six years old. I was put to bed right after the meal but I couldn't fall asleep. When I heard everyone singing all those wonderful songs, I was miserable because I wasn't part of the festivities. I was too well brought up to run out there in my nightclothes and join them, but I swore to myself that I would never again go to bed before the Seder was finished. And I never did.

I remember that Grosspapa conducted the Seder in his white robe. He sat in a large upholstered armchair covered with a white sheet, and he reclined on a white, covered bed pillow for his back. The *Hagadah* says, "Be comfortably reclined," and Grosspapa certainly was.

I always sat next to him and knew that he was hiding the *Afikomen* under the sheet on the armrest.

"Do you know what the *Affikomen* is?" he would ask.

"Sure, it's a piece of matzoh!" one of the children would say.

"You are right," he would answer. "You saw me wrapping it up.

When you find it, I will cut it into little pieces for our dessert. No sweets tonight. Nothing after the *Affikomen!*"

Then, like today, if you found the *Affikomen* you got a present. I would slowly move my hand under the bed sheet, hoping that Grosspapa was so involved in conducting the Seder that he wouldn't notice. But just as I sensed I was getting close to the *Affikomen*, I would feel a slight slap on my hand and Grosspapa would push the wrapped matzoh back under the sheet.

He would never miss a beat reading from the *Hagadah*, acting as if nothing had happened, but the grin on his face revealed that he, too, was playing the game. After a while, I would try again, but the *Affikomen* would be long gone! For a moment, when I wasn't looking, Grosspapa had quickly hidden it somewhere else. Eventually, one of the children would find it, get the present, and we would all sing "Shir Hamalot" in a special Passover melody, and then we chanted the Grace After the Meal.

They would fill up the wine glasses for the last time and open the door to the hallway to let the prophet Elijah enter, and then came my favorite part of the whole evening, the singing of the more traditional songs.

Both sets of grandparents, and my parents too, took great time and trouble to carefully pass on the rich traditions of our faith. Anything else would have been unthinkable--they were, after all, the patriarchs and matriarchs and honored their Jewish heritage as they expected their children would continue to do. I am indebted and eternally grateful to them, not just for the happiest of childhood memories, but for the richness and comfort that my enduring faith has given to my life.

Chapter VI
My Parents

My mother was dancing on a tabletop when my father first laid eyes on her. She was showing off to her friends at a Jewish organization dance. She was sixteen, a beautiful and vivacious girl, a tiny doll, only about five feet tall, with light brown, curly hair, bright gray eyes, and a cute curvy figure with dynamite legs. Daddy was instantly smitten and fell in love right away.

Selma Böninger was born on December 30, 1898. My father, Hellmuth, met her when he was eighteen. She had graduated from the Jewish high school for girls with very good grades, but her real love was music and singing. She had a good soprano voice and she wanted one day to sing in the opera.

My grandparents Böninger wouldn't hear of it. A nice Jewish girl from a good family did not belong on the stage and they would under no circum-

Selma Böninger

stances finance studies for such an unrespectable career. This was not negotiable, so my mother decided to try her hand at fashion.

She loved clothes and she was very good at sketching. Fashion design appealed to her, but she first had to become a dressmaker, so she started as an apprentice in one of the better dressmaking shops in Hamburg.

At that time, ready-made, off the rack clothing did not exist, of course. Poor people made their own clothes, and the more affluent went to dressmakers. These shops had all the latest magazines showing the newest "haute couture" fashions from Paris. Clients would select a style, and then a dressmaker would design a custom pattern according to the customer's measurements.

Some shops carried their own fabrics and trimmings, but the women often bought their material in one of the many specialty shops around *Neuer Wall* in Hamburg, or they would bring the silks and wools back from travels in Italy or France. After various fittings, the garments usually turned out to be very attractive.

A new apprentice started with menial jobs like sweeping the floor and keeping the place tidy. After a while, they were taught to sew and to make patterns, and, much later, they assisted in the fittings.

My mother was not very happy with this tedious, ground level beginning to her new career, but later in her life these basic skills came in very handy.

My father, after graduating at eighteen from the *Oberrealschule Eppendorf*, the equivalent of our high school and college, was apprenticed to a dealer of new and old ferrous metals. In Germany, everybody had to go through a two- or three-year apprenticeship before being accepted as a regular employee in any commercial establishment. Daddy had decided to become a businessman, and the training at the metal company was a good beginning for his career.

Daddy's plans were cut short after the assassination of Archduke Franz Ferdinand of the Austro-Hungarian Empire by a Serbian nationalist in Sarajevo. The First World War began on August 1, 1914, when Germany declared war on Russia and then two days later declared war on France.

My father, like most German Jews, had been brought up to be a patriotic German citizen, and he volunteered for the Army. He started in the infantry and later advanced, eventually becoming a *Hussar*, part of a prestigious regiment easily recognized by their distinct steel, bell-shaped helmets with multicolored plumage. Pictures show Hellmuth as a handsome young man in this regalia.

Selma and Hellmuth decided they would get married at the end of the war, and on one

Hellmuth Schragenheim in Hussar uniform

of his furloughs, in 1916, my parents got engaged. My mother's parents, Mery and Moritz Böninger, were very happy with this development. Hellmuth was from a good, solid Jewish family that was well-established and well-regarded in Hamburg's Jewish society. He had good manners and was well groomed, intelligent, and ambitious. He was very charming and Selma was obviously in love with him. He was also a good talker; indeed, he talked a lot, perhaps too much! "Don't you think you should go home?" my grandmother would say when it became very late in the evening, and he was still chatting away in the Böninger's living room.

On the other hand, Hellmuth's mother, Claire Schragenheim, was terribly disappointed with the match. Hellmuth, her first-born, was the apple of his mother's eye. She thought he was too young--not yet established in any career or business--just a vulnerable soldier in love with a young girl back home.

She wanted him to marry a "society girl," the daughter of a rich and distinguished Jewish family, possibly the daughter of one of the many Jewish bankers, ship owners, or renowned Jewish doctors or lawyers. In her eyes, the Böningers were much too middle class and too informal in their lifestyle, just not good enough for her Prince Hellmuth, her cherished son whom she treated like he was one of the reigning Hohenzollerns.

Every time Hellmuth came home on a furlough, his mother would say to him, "Hellmuth, in synagogue I saw the younger daughter of the so-and-so's. What a beautiful girl she is, Hellmuth! Hellmuth, her mother said to me that they would like their daughter to meet you. Why don't you let me arrange a meeting?"

But Hellmuth could not be persuaded by his mother to give up Selma. Because of Claire Schragenheim's feelings for the Böninger family and for her future daughter-in-law, the relationship between the two women never was very good. They tolerated each other and managed to get along, but the Schragenheims and the Böningers never socialized and would only get together for weddings, special birthdays, or other formal functions when not to do so would have obviously been a social insult.

The pictures of the engagement party show a radiant young couple, my mother enchantingly lovely and my young father absolutely impressive in his military garb.

Selma Böninger's and Hellmuth Schragenheim's engagement, 1916

The following year, my father was injured in a battle in France, near Verdun. The family was told that he suffered a head wound. Overcoming their tense feelings for each other, my mother and Hellmuth's mother secured permission to travel together to visit their beloved, wounded Hellmuth at a field hospital. Travel during wartime, especially in enemy territory, was tricky and when they finally reached the small town in France where the regiment had been stationed, they found the soldiers had left just minutes before on a march to the Russian Front.

No one had any information about wounded soldiers, so the women took off after the regiment, looking for Hellmuth. They caught up with the men and ran along the ranks of soldiers looking at every face, asking about Hellmuth Schragenheim, but neither did they see him nor did anyone know about him.

By then, they were completely exhausted, physically and emotionally, and both collapsed at the side of the road and wept. After a while, they sensed there was nothing they could do but go back into the town and continue searching; after many more questions, they finally found Hellmuth in a small field hospital.

His head was completely swathed in bandages, but he was otherwise well; he was both surprised and delighted to see "his two women," and he pronounced them the best medicine he could get. He said he considered himself lucky, having sustained only a scalp wound; what's more, the doctor was holding him for a while to get his strength back, so he had a temporary reprieve from the war. He'd already been transferred to another regiment by the time the armistice ending the war was signed on November 11, 1918, and shortly after that he was discharged from the army.

On August 24, 1919, the Chief Rabbi of Hamburg married Selma and Hellmuth in the big synagogue on *Bornplatz*. As was the custom, the wedding dinner was at the Böningers' house. I often asked my mother to describe the details to me. The table was decorated in white and lilac with beautiful arrangements of different kinds of lilac flowers. Lilac was my mother's favorite color; she always wore a lot of lilac, and used the color often in her decorating.

Dowries were still very common in those years. Not only did the parents of the bride provide for the wedding, but they also bought all the furniture for the young couple's apartment, as well as all the linens and towels, usually all hand-embroidered with the bride's new monogram. They also gave dishes, glasses, and sterling silver flatware engraved with the first initial of the bride's married name.

A complete set of dishes for a proper, middle class Jewish household consisted of four complete sets: everyday dishes with one set for *milchig* and another set for *fleischig* and so-called "good dishes," one set *milchig* and another set *fleischig*, for holidays and entertaining. The same applied to the flatware, which was usually silver-plated for everyday use and sterling silver for more festive occasions.

In addition to all these household necessities, there was usually a substantial sum of money given by the bride's father to the bride-groom. Today, the dowry idea smacks of a cattle deal or an auction where the father pays the groom to take his daughter off his hands-- and it might have been true in some cases, where the daughter was an unattractive old maid--but this was certainly not the case as far as my mother was concerned: she was young and she was beautiful.

The Böningers were considered good, middle class people and Grosspapa was well established in his wholesale business of hair and beauty supplies, but they were not wealthy. This was quite an outlay, and poor grandfather Böninger had yet another daughter to worry about; Bianka, their oldest daughter, was not married yet, and he would soon have to provide her dowry, too.

After the wedding, my parents went right to their lovely apartment on *Martinistrasse* in the *Eppendorf* section of Hamburg to spend their wedding night. The day after the wedding, the whole family came for coffee and cake and spent the afternoon with them admiring their new home.

In those years, even a young couple just starting out would live in a rather spacious apartment. They had a living room, dining room, and library, as well as two bedrooms, plus a maid's room and a balcony. Grossmama Böninger had also hired a sleep-in maid for them and had bought her the usual uniforms, which consisted of long-sleeved, black or gray cotton dresses with white cuffs and collars, plus a little white half apron and a white cap. Mother told me that the maid was young and cute and served the young couple delicious breakfasts on the balcony when the weather was good.

Their married life began. Daddy started working for Grosspapa in his wholesale toiletries and beauty supplies business, and Mutti became a homemaker. She shopped and tried her best to cook all of her husband's favorite foods. She fixed up her apartment, made her home as beautiful as she could, and met her friends every afternoon for coffee and cake in one of the many Konditorein (pastry shops) in Hamburg. Three months later, she became pregnant with me, and everyone in the family eagerly awaited the arrival of the new baby.

Selma and Hellmuth Schragenheim, Hamburg, Germany

Chapter VII
My Early Childhood

A ugust 24th 1920 was my parent's first wedding anniversary. I was their present. I was born that day.

I was brought into this world at the *Vereinshospital, Beim Schlump*, a small hospital located in what was then a residential neighborhood in Hamburg.

My mother had planned to name me Inge--a very popular name at that time--but as Mutti lay there in the hospital she could

Baby Margot

hear people talking outside on the street, and it seemed to her that every young girl in Hamburg was named Inge. "I i n g e e, come up for lunch" or "I i n g e e, don't cross the street." She heard the mothers constantly calling Inge, stretching out the name in the typical Hamburg pronunciation, and she quickly got tired of Inge, and named me Margot instead.

My middle name was Berta, after my great-grandmother, Berta Enoch née Wolff, the mother of my father's mother, Claire. Dear great-grandmother Berta, who was eighty-nine, had awaited the birth of her first great-grandchild with holy expectation, but, unfortunately, she died right before I was born. (I never liked my middle name and as dear as my great-grandmother must have been, I dropped Berta as soon as I got to America.)

Margot

Pictures show me as a pretty, chubby, little baby with dark hair and alert eyes, and apparently nobody was too disappointed that I was not a boy.

My mother said I cried a lot, and as she was young and inexperienced she didn't know what to do about it. She probably did not have enough milk for me. When Grossmama Böninger came to visit, she took one look at me, and said, "I know what's wrong with her, Selma. She's hungry."

She went into the kitchen, made a puree of carrots, put me on her lap, and gave me my first "real" food. I stopped crying immediately. Grossmama said, "I was right. She knows you love her, darling, but that child was hungry." She ever-so-sweetly told my mother how to start feeding me and, presumably, it took care of my crying and my crankiness.

I was an only child for the first four years of my life, and everyone doted on me. That changed when my mother became pregnant again and was due to have her second child in the summer of 1924.

I remember an incident during the last part of her pregnancy when we took the streetcar to visit a relative. The streetcar was crowded but someone got up to offer Mutti his place. With her big belly, it was hard for my mother to squeeze into the seat. I watched this struggle and then commented quite loudly, "Mutti, if you hadn't eaten so many potatoes you would have been able to fit!" Even at the age of four, I was rather outspoken.

In anticipation of the new baby, my parents moved into a larger apartment, *Nissenstrasse 14*, which was also in *Eppendorf.* I remember the apartment quite well because we stayed there until I was in my early teens. It was on the main floor of the building and the living room was to the left of the front door. I remember big armchairs, upholstered in a formal purple and gold striped fabric. The dining room had dark oak furniture, and from that room two glass doors led into the *Herrenzimmer* (library); every good German family had a library. There were rooms on both sides of the long, narrow corridor. One was my parents' bedroom, and the other was my sister's room. My room was all the way at the end of the hallway, and my window overlooked the back garden. Our large kitchen also looked out at the garden. Of course, there were maids' rooms and bathrooms. One of the rooms I liked the best was the sewing room. Once a month, a seamstress came to repair any damaged bed and table linens and to do minor alterations.

When it was cold, coal-burning stoves provided heat. They were in every room, and in the formal rooms the stoves were covered with decorative tiles on the outside to make them prettier. Early every morning during the winter, the maid would fill all the stoves with coal and light the fires, and during the day she would add coals so the fires didn't go out. But during the night, the coals would die down, and it would get very cold, indeed; we slept under puffy down comforters and stayed as warm as we could until the fires were started up again in the morning.

There were no washing machines in homes back then. The maid washed our underwear, blouses, and other delicate things, but once a week, or once every two weeks, our very large laundress came to do the heavy laundry, and it was quite a production.

Everyday life was more formal then and tablecloths and cloth napkins were used all the time (that added up to a lot of laundry). On wash day, those table linens and all the towels and bed clothes were boiled in huge pots with special laundry soap, the massive laundress stirring the huge laundry pots with large wooden spoons. I would sit in the kitchen watching her every move as she emptied the scalding water into a deep, divided laundry sink. With the steam billowing around her, she poked the laundry with the spoon handles and lifted up each steaming article, looking with her eagle eye for any stubborn spots that hadn't come out in the boiling. Humming to herself, or singing to me, she scrubbed the stubborn spots out on a wooden washboard with an aluminum grill in front.

She rinsed everything a few times, and then with her incredibly strong forearms and hands she squeezed every last drop of water out of everything. She propped the laundry basket on her hip and trudged the loads out into the garden to dry on lines strung from special poles. She came back the next day to do all the ironing.

July 14, 1924, is as clear to me today as it was so many years ago. I'd been watching the laundress as she turned our kitchen into a sauna when suddenly Uncle Bruno burst into the room. He was my father's only brother, younger and still unmarried, very fair with curly, blond hair and blue-blue eyes, the opposite of my father's coloring.

Uncle Bruno picked me up and said, "Well, little one, you have a beautiful baby sister! Mutti is in the hospital with the new baby and she sends you a big kiss." He then took me to Grossmutti and Grossvati, who were vacationing at the beach. Off we went to *Travemuende*, my first trip on a train, and I recall that when we got there we sat on the beach all dressed up in our regular street clothes. That was the day Vera was born.

My father had wanted a son. Optimistically, my parents had picked out the name Werner for their new child. When the baby turned out to be another girl, the closest girl's name to Werner was Vera and that is how she got her name.

The first time I saw my sister, my mother put little Vera in my arms and said to me, "Here, Margot, is your little sister. You must promise me that you will always take good care of her for the rest of your life." Her words have stayed with me, and, in fact, Vera said to me recently, "You must have listened to what Mutti said because you have truly taken very good care of me all your life."

My first conscious memory of Vera is corroborated by a photograph, which was probably taken the next spring. It was taken in our garden and little Vera is sitting on the lap of the nursemaid. I do vividly remember her curly, white-blonde hair and her big, blue eyes. To me, she looked like an incredibly cute, life-sized doll, and I was captivated by her.

Like most little girls, I had a huge collection of dolls and stuffed animals. I wanted to share my treasures with my little sister, especially when she was cooped up in her playpen, so I used to give her one of my dolls to play with. For some unknown reason, Vera would grab the doll from me, throw it on the floor of the playpen, and then trample it viciously with her tiny feet.

I initially thought that it was because she didn't like what I'd chosen to give her, so I tried to give her other dolls and stuffed animals, but the results were always the same. This sisterly ritual always ended the same way. I would cry and try to retrieve my toys, but that would make Vera scream even more. Mutti or the nursemaid would have to calm us down. I don't know

Vera and Margo

79

why my sister, who turned out to be such an easy-going, mild-mannered person, was so feisty as a small child, but I'm glad that those outbursts of unbecoming temper early on never diminished my love for her.

Later, we had a new nursemaid. She was wonderful. She must have truly loved children. She had been trained at the *Fröbel School*, which was founded by the renowned Dr. Friedrich Wilhelm August Fröbel during the previous century. He was a highly respected educator and the founder of the kindergarten system.

As little as I was, I remember this nursemaid fondly. She had found her calling because she played with us so sweetly and gave us her devoted attention. She built a terrific doll house for us made of decorated cardboard, and she showed us how to make furniture for the house: little paper arm chairs and sofas. She helped us make flowers out of crepe paper and wire, and taught us how to fold colored sheets of paper into the shape of little sailboats. She made us delicious treats, like slices of blood oranges with chocolate on top and small pieces of cake with chocolate sprinkles.

Mutti sometimes joined us during these afternoon play-times, and when the nursemaid had her day off and the weather was nice, Mutti would take us to the *Stadtpark*, a large park about a ten-minute walk from our apartment. The park was filled with beautiful old trees, lawns, and walkways, and had three or four restaurants with outdoor gardens. We would drink a sparkling fruit drink called *Brause*, similar to our sodas, but a little less bubbly. Mutti played all kinds of games with us on the lawn. I still see her running and laughing with us. She was in her twenties and full of pep and energy.

One of the games I remember particularly well was called in Italian, *Fra Diavolo* or "Between the Devil." The game is derived from the Chinese yo-yo. A diabolo, also known as "the devil on two sticks," is a juggling prop consisting of a rubber spool which is whirled on a string tied to two sticks held one in each hand. If you were experienced at the game, you could do lots of tricks with the sticks, and Mutti was very, very good at it. She could toss the diabolo overhead and catch it as it came down on the string and all the while keep it spinning.

Chapter VIII
A Comfortable Life

My parents adored each other. I can't remember them ever having an argument or raising their voices. Daddy called Mutti "Muschi" or "Muschilein" and Daddy was called "Puschi" or "Schatzi." They loved to social-ize and we always had lots of company at our house. I can still remember listening to my mother's laughter in the living room while I was in my bed.

Selma and Hellmuth Schragenheim

From the time I was born un-til the time Hitler came to power in 1933, the life of a Jewish mid-dle class woman in Germany was easy and pleasurable. A nursemaid took care of the children, a maid did the cleaning and served the meals, and the laundress washed the clothes. In the morning, Mutti would go to the market to buy fresh food for the day. She then came home and cooked. We ate our main meal at 1:00 p.m., and Daddy would usually come home to eat unless he was out of town. After eating, Daddy and Mutti would both take naps and then Daddy would return to his place of work.

In the afternoon, Mutti would meet friends for a game of bridge, or they would gather at a pleasant coffee house for coffee and pastries. The women would shop together, take little boat rides on the Alster River, visit museums, attend recitals, or just visit at each other's homes.

While we were small, we were always served our evening meal by the nursemaid and then put to bed. Our evening meals were simple, just a sandwich with a glass of milk and a pudding or some fruit with a cookie for dessert. The adults ate around 7:30 or 8:00 p.m., and when we were older we ate with them. Evening meals were simple, too: a platter of cold cuts with a variety of breads and lots of butter or some frankfurters with homemade potato salad or perhaps an omelet with some fried potatoes. Only on Friday nights, holidays, or other special occasions were full course dinners served at night.

The summer I turned six, Mutti said to me, "The time has come for you to take swimming lessons." Mutti had never learned how to swim, and she had made up her mind that her children would be swimmers. Hamburg was built around and along water and it was smart to be able to stay afloat.

The *Alster*, a small, narrow river in the suburbs, widened in the center of the city and looked more like a lake. It was called the *Aussenalster*. The *Binnenalster*, which was much smaller, almost a square, flowed into the Elbe from the old part of the city. The *Elbe* is one of the big rivers of Germany; it starts in the mountains of Saxony and flows into the North Sea. It carried all kinds of commercial barges, overseas freighters, and passenger ships. The Hamburg harbor is still one of the largest in Europe with enormous storage and shipbuilding facilities. Obviously, someone living in Hamburg needed to know how to swim.

One warm spring day, Mutti took me to the open-air swimming pool in our neighborhood, which was called *Lattenkamp*.

Mutti had hired a young, blonde swimming teacher to give me private lessons. She showed me the leg and arm movements on dry land, lying on my belly on a cot. Then she tied three, flexible cork belts around me and lowered me into the water in an alarming looking, harness-like contraption that terrified me. Her plan was to ease me out of this supporting basket and tow me around the pool suspended by the cork floats while I held onto long bamboo sticks. We never got that far. The poles broke and I started to scream, disrupting the whole pool full of people, who cheered loudly when the beleaguered teacher finally lifted me out of the water.

My mother, however, was not going to be denied. I was going to learn to swim no matter what, and she was smart enough to know I shouldn't be allowed to leave the pool traumatized. She comforted me and said softly to me,

"Margot, I don't want you to be afraid of the water. Water will always carry you. Right now, you have corks, which will help until you really can swim. I will show you how wonderful these floats can be."

She went with me into the shallow part of the pool where both of us could stand, and she spread her arms out in front of her and bent down on her knees. "Now I want you to lie flat on my arms and move your legs and your arms like the teacher told you to." I did what she said. I trusted her completely. We practiced this part, then when she had me relaxed and having a good time she said, "Now I will show you how to float on your own just holding onto my hands, okay? I'm right here and you can hold onto me. You'll be fine."

My mother succeeded where the teacher had failed. I was at home in the water. How clever she was to have won me over. Eventually I took some "official" lessons and became a good swimmer.

Certificate from *Lattenkamp* Swimming Pool, Hamburg, Germany

Daddy, or Pappi as we called him, had quit working for Gross-papa during the first year of his marriage. He found a job as a salesman in one of the high-class cigar and tobacco stores on *Jungfernstieg*, which to this day is still one of the finest shopping streets in Hamburg, its shops facing the picturesque riverfront. The owner of the cigar store taught Daddy the business. He was looking for a reliable young man who could be groomed as his successor. Daddy was an excellent salesman and learned quickly.

Shortly after Daddy started work there, Germany found itself mired in the horrible inflation that people still talk about today. The value of money changed every day, and the purchasing power of the German mark was so diminished that 1000 marks would only buy a loaf of bread. Mutti later told me that every night she would meet Daddy at the store with a suitcase which they filled with his day's earnings. Usually white collar workers were paid monthly, but this was no longer possible because of how the value of money changed on a daily basis. In any case, they would have needed a cart to carry a month's worth of paper money. They would take the streetcar or a taxi to the stores near our apartment and buy as much food as they could with the money in the suitcase. The next day, the same amount of money bought even less. Money was being printed in enormous quantities, in incredibly high denominations, and was hardly worth the paper it was printed on. People who had a lot of money lost fortunes, but somehow Mutti and Daddy, as well as the families Schragenheim and Böninger, managed to survive. They lived as well as any upper middle class family could live from the time I was six, in 1926, to a few years immediately after Hitler came to power.

Daddy did well at the shop and after working a year or two, he was asked to become a salesman for *Attika* cigarettes, part of *Reemstma*, the largest cigarette manufacturer in Germany at that time and owned mostly by Jews. They had a special division that produced only the Attika brand. Daddy was soon made the district manager for a large territory, taking in Hamburg and its surroundings, and parts of the provinces of *Mecklenburg* and *Schleswig-Holstein*. He was given a Mercedes with a uniformed chauffeur who drove him around town or away on business trips. Daddy was only in his early thirties and was deservedly proud of his responsible and prestigious position.

Hellmuth Schragenheim with Mercedes automobile and chauffeur outside Hamburg

PART II

Chapter IX

Starting School

In 1927, just after Easter, I became pupil number 3240 at the *Israelitische Toecherschule* (School for Jewish Girls), located on Karolinenstrasse, in the St. Pauli District of Hamburg. I began studying Hebrew, Jewish history, and Jewish rituals, in addition to the regular curriculum of a German school.

The state subsidized Jewish schools and they had to adhere to the curriculum of the Hamburg school board, but tuition was based on the income of the father of the pupil. In other words, a child from a very poor family did not have to pay anything, while the richest paid the most.

My parents would have preferred to enroll me in one of the many good schools in our neighborhood, but both sides of the family pressured them to enroll me in the Jewish school my mother had graduated from, even though *Karolinenstrasse* was a long way from where we lived. I had to walk to the terminal of Streetcar #24, which took about 10 to 15 minutes, and then ride for about 30 to 40 minutes to the stop in front of the school.

A child had to be at least six years old to start school, but my parents had tried to enroll me in 1926 despite the fact that I was four months shy of my sixth birthday. They told the admitting office that I was very precocious and could easily keep pace with the other children, but the rules could not bent for little Margot.

Margot on her first day of school,
April 1927

Now my time had come and I was thrilled. On the first day, I wore my sailor's outfit: a middy blouse, navy blue skirt, a white shirt, and a full length navy coat with a regular sailor's collar and black sailor's tie. I had on a jaunty sailor's cap with a ribbon with the name of a popular navy vessel inscribed in gold letters. Cotton stockings and patent leather shoes completed the outfit. I was ready for my first great adventure.

I also had a *Schultüte*, which literally translated means a school paper bag but actually is a cardboard tube covered with fancy paper. Mine was gold with little rosebud decorations. The *Schultüte* was filled with candies for everyone in the class. In addition, I carried a small shoulder bag with an identification name tag to hold my lunch, and on my back I wore a *Raentzel*, a leather backpack shaped like a brief case for holding my textbooks, notebooks, and other essentials, a lot of equipment for such a little girl. I was proud of myself. At six years old, I was ready to make my own decisions.

Outside the classroom, the mothers prepared to turn over their excited and frightened children to the teacher, Rebecka Weissmann, a very kind, motherly, soft-spoken woman. To me, she seemed middle aged but she was probably only in her thirties. She had dark, brown hair pulled back into a tight chignon and kind, brown eyes. She made us feel very welcomed and comfortable when we entered her classroom.

We sat at small desks, two of them side by side, according to her seating chart; there were about 25 of us, and she had us each stand up when she read our names.

These many years later, I can recall only a few of the girls from the school, but I distinctly remember Alice Baruch, who became my best friend, and I remember Inge Stiefel, who also became part of our "inner circle."

I also remember Uschi Brager. In fact, it was a few years later when Uschi Brager was transferred to our school that we formed our inseparable "four leaf clover inner circle." We were ten years old by then, and Alice, Inge, and I took an immediate liking to Uschi, the new, beautiful girl with the big blue eyes and long blonde curls. We became inseparable. Alice, who lived in California, is dead, and Inge, who settled in London, is also gone.

Alice, Margot, and Marion, bottom row

But we lost Marion Weil, the prettiest of us all, at a very young age. I also remember Edith Engers, who I still saw in my early years in New York but who I lost track of later on. Uschi has lived in Los Angeles for many years.

We attended school six days a week because we covered more subjects than the regular German schools. Of course, Jewish schools were closed Saturdays, and nobody was very happy about going to school on Sundays but we did. The regular school day, however, was short. We started at eight and ended no later than one. There were no classes in the afternoons. We all belonged to Jewish sports clubs, and, of course, there were never any activities on Shabbat. Many of our sports activities--games and practices--were on Sunday.

I loved going to school and I continued to love learning even as I grew older. I very seldom missed school, except when I came down with the various childhood illnesses like chicken pox, measles, and whooping cough. I liked going to school so much that I was even glad when school vacations were over.

Mutti brought me to school and picked me up on the first day, and she then made arrangements with another mother who lived within walking distance of the school to put me on the streetcar every day when school was over. After school, Mutti or the maid would then pick me up from the terminal and walk me home. I was fearless and I was not afraid to travel alone although it was a long trip for a young child. Things went along well for a while until one day I missed finding the woman who usually put me on the streetcar home. I thought I was so grown up that I could find my way by myself. "I know Streetcar #24," I said to myself. "All I have to do is go to the last stop." When the streetcar pulled up, I got on and told the conductor to take me to the last stop.

"Sure, little one," he said, "I'll take you to the last stop." I was very proud of myself, and I sat next to a window and looked out. "I don't need anyone," I thought. After a short while, I noticed that the streets were unfamiliar and I realized that something was wrong. I went back to the conductor and said, "Are you sure this streetcar is going to the last stop in *Eppendorf?*" "Oh, my G-d," he said, "You're going the wrong way. We're going in the opposite direction." When he saw me panic, he said, "Don't worry. Here's what we'll do. I will go to the end of the line, then turn around. Just stay on and I'll take you all the way back to the last stop in *Eppendorf.*"

Actually, I was having a good time. I thought it was a great adventure. It never occurred to me how worried my mother must have been when I didn't get off the streetcar at the regular time. When I finally got to the *Eppendorf* terminal, Mutti and the maid were waiting. Both were frantic, both were crying. They began hugging me and scolding me at the same time.

They had called the school and the police and the woman who was supposed to put me on the streetcar, and nobody--not a soul--knew where I was. After all the excitement was over, Mutti explained to me that I had forgotten to cross the street in order to get the correct streetcar going in the right direction. She told me to be more careful in the future, to cross the street with other kids and adults when school was over, and to make sure I got on the #24 to *Eppendorf*. I never lost my way again. I was, indeed, becoming independent.

When I was young, I was always picked up by someone who walked me home, but when I got older I became the proud owner of a bicycle. After that, I rode to school every day, no matter what kind of weather. Hamburg is known for its many rainy days, and the saying goes that every Hamburg child is born with a raincoat. On real rainy days, I'd put on a raincoat, but often I just could not be bothered and I sat in school in my wet clothes. At that point in my life, it really didn't matter. I didn't have a care in the world.

Margot's Report Card, December 1930, age 10

Chapter X
The Death of Marion Weil

My school friend Marion Weil's death at the age of ten deeply affected me. I vividly remember the details. I remember exactly what happened. I suddenly realized how fragile my carefree life really was.

Marion was one of the prettiest girls in our class. She was a little chubby and had a round face and short, blonde, straight hair with bangs across her forehead; she had big, blue eyes. She looked very much like a big "Kaete Kruse Puppe," still

Marion Weil

Germany's best known doll. Marion told us that her parents were contemplating divorce and that they were fighting about which parent would have custody of her. She confided in a few of her closest friends that she was very unhappy and that she did not know what to do.

"I love them both so very much," she would say. "So how can I choose between them?

"Besides, my Mutti is all alone. My mother's parents are not alive anymore and she has no brothers or sisters, while Vati (as she called her father) has a large family. But I would also miss him so." Joint custody was unheard of at that time. The Weils solved their problem in a different way.

One morning when we arrived at school, we were told that Marion had died. We found out that her parents had turned on the gas in their kitchen and all three of them were found by the police, dead in each other's arms. Perhaps, in the end, they were spared a worse fate later on in Hitler's gas chambers, but at that time, in 1930, it was by far the greatest tragedy in our young lives.

Chapter XI
Daddy's Business

I still remember seeing Paul von Hindenburg ride by in a big open Mercedes, his motorcade driving through the streets of Hamburg, crowds cheering him from either side. He was a nice-looking, old gentleman with his white hair and big white mustache.

Like the rest of the world, Germany felt the effects of the American stock market crash of 1929 and the subsequent depression. The world was shrinking even then, and there was severe unemployment and discontent in my country. The working classes were looking to the political extreme left or to the extreme right for salvation.

Communists and other leftist political parties argued about unifying the working class, and Adolf Hitler and his cronies led the burgeoning National Socialists, also known as the Nazis.

Hitler was a charismatic, powerful, and persuasive speaker who promised the German people that he would make them supreme and successful and rich again.

Seventy-five years later, I can still hear his voice, harsh and caustic, sometimes screaming in a high pitch--it gives me chills-- and I can hear the voices of the crowds he was wooing, masses of people cheering him on.

Germany's government was brought to a standstill. Hindenburg was persuaded by his advisers to make Hitler Chancellor of

Germany, which would, in turn, permit him to run the government. I doubt many know it, but Hitler was sworn in on January 30, 1933, the exact same day FDR was sworn in for his first term as President of the United States. I have always thought this bit of trivia an especially poignant and strange coincidence of history.

Because of the deteriorating economic conditions in Germany, the *Reemstma* Tobacco Company, where Daddy worked, decided to consolidate their operations. Daddy was the general sales agent for Northern Germany for *Reemstma's* cigarette brand, *Attikah*. After consolidating their operations, Remstma no longer needed regional agents for their various brands. I don't know whether or not they offered Daddy a different job in their organization, but he made the surprising decision to start his own wholesale business in cigarettes, cigars, and tobaccos. In retrospect, it would seem a strange choice for a Jew during that period to establish a new business. However, while times were somewhat unsettled, Hitler had not yet become Chancellor, and Daddy, believe it or not, began his business in 1932.

Daddy found a loft with an adjoining office in *Eppendorf*, not too far from our apartment, and he proudly put up an engraved copper plaque next to the entrance door of the building,

HELLMUTH SCHRAGENHEIM
TABAKWAREN- GROSSHANDEL
(Wholesaler of Tobacco Goods)

He had special shelves built for the variety of merchandise. There was a huge packing table with wrapping material, and next to it was his nicely furnished office. Daddy bought a car for himself (a lovely little BMW) and a delivery van. He hired a driver to make deliveries, a helper, and an apprentice. Actually, he became quite successful. From his many years of experience in this field, he knew the merchandise and he knew his customers. In fact, Daddy was an excellent salesman with a wonderful, outgoing personality; his customers loved him. At that time, there were tobacco stores on almost every street corner in Hamburg, and there were stores in the smaller towns in the surrounding areas. His favorite customers, however, were restaurants and nightclubs. They always bought the highest priced cigarettes and the best cigars, and he and Mutti enjoyed the fringe benefits: dinners and shows in the various nightclubs he sold to.

During school vacations--or after school hours during the busy season--Vera and I helped in the business. Daddy showed us how to arrange the stock. The cigarettes came from the factories in big paper-covered bundles shaped like huge cubes. The bundles were unwrapped and packages of cigarettes were placed on the shelves, starting with the cheapest, 2-1/2 Pfennig per cigarette (the smallest package had four cigarettes and could be bought for 10 Pfennig). Next came the 3-1/3 Pfennig cigarette (the smallest package contained six cigarettes and sold for 20 Pfennig), and so on and so on, to the most expensive cigarettes, 10-1/2 Pfennig each, sold only in packages of 20 cigarettes.

Cigars of all shapes and colors were sold in wood boxes of 10, 20, or 50, and, of course, there was a full stock of pipe and chewing tobacco. Vera had great fun filling small plastic bags with chewing tobacco; this required using tongs to pick clumps of it out of a big earthenware jar and filling 10 or 20 bags, depending on the size of the order. My specialty was making packages. Daddy's helper would assemble the order from our inventory, putting all the different packs of cigarettes on the long wooden table. Daddy showed me how to estimate the size of paper I needed, how to tear off the sheets from the paper dispenser, and how to fabricate a nice square package, and seal it with paper tape. I became an expert packer, and even now I still think of Daddy's store every time I produce a perfect package out of odd items.

But what I remember the most was the smell of tobacco in the storage room. Daddy kept the tobacco moist by an ingenious system of hanging damp cloths at night. Aged, cured tobacco has a fragrance as wonderful as perfume.

When I lived in New York, I used to love going with Henry to Dunhill's on Fifth Avenue. I'd go into their humidor where they kept cigars and tobacco, and the smell transported me back to Hamburg and to our storage loft. The same thing happens to Vera. She said she once went into a little store in Toledo that had a smoking section and a humidor. She told the clerk she just wanted to go in for a smell. He looked at her like she was crazy. She explained about Daddy's business and told him that she wasn't nuts; she just wanted to take a little olfactory trip back in time. He laughed and told her to go in and sniff away!

Tobacco wholesaling turned out to be a good business until the government started controlling prices and left too small a margin for a wholesaler to exist profitably. The government aimed to obliterate wholesalers. They thought that if factories sold directly to retailers, prices would drop and people would be able to buy more, enabling Germany to get out of its recession faster. Daddy countered by expanding his high-end cigar business and concentrating on the higher priced and the imported cigarettes. I loved the cigarettes made in Russia, very thin with very long paper filters. Daddy continued selling tobacco as long as he could until it became impossible for Jews to do any business in Germany.

Chapter XII
Discovering (More Than) Boys

I discovered boys at the age of twelve. My first boyfriend (if you can call it that) was exactly my age, the son of friends of my parents. He was a good-looking kid with curly, blond hair and big, blue eyes. It was innocent enough. We went for walks in the parks and as a sign of his affection he would give me a little peck on the cheek each time we met or said goodbye. But a friend had shown him how to smoke and he insisted I try it, too. We sat on a park bench and he lit a cigarette and showed me how to puff so that the light would keep going and not go out. Then he showed me how to inhale. Boy, did I start coughing.

When we saw one of the strict park security officers, we would cover our cigarettes with our hollow hands to make sure no smoke could escape, and we pretended we were engaged in serious conversation. Needless to say, we burned our hands. I also burned my eyelashes and my eyebrows trying to light cigarettes. Still, I continued experimenting with smoking at home when my parents were out and our maid was gone for the day. I made Vera promise that she would never tell anyone about my smoking. I would open all the windows in the house, even on the coldest winter evenings, so that there would be no tell-tale odor when my parents came home. In spite of all this, my father eventually found out about my smoking. He sat me down for a serious talk and explained to me how bad it was for a growing child to smoke, but he promised me that I would be allowed to smoke as soon as I graduated from school. "Then, I will give you one pack of Attikah cigarettes per week," he said. "There are 20 cigarettes in a pack and you may smoke at home after dinner or with your friends. But you have to promise me not to buy any more cigarettes now and not to smoke again until then." We both kept our promises.

Many of my friends were not allowed to smoke, but they smoked like crazy anyway; I, on the other hand, just smoked a few cigarettes and kept my smoking habit under control. Because it was not a forbidden fruit, it was not that exciting to me. Later on, after I'd left home, I smoked a lot more but at least I was prevented from doing so when I was very, very young.

Hitler was now Chancellor and Jews were prevented from leading normal lives. He made frequent speeches about the "pure German race" and about "the conspiracy of the international Jewish community." You could hear his speeches on the radio, and the enthusiastic cheers and applause of the audience were frightening. Columns of SA men in their brown uniforms and caps, swastikas on their lapels, marched through the streets, as did columns of Hitler youths. They marched in goose step, singing their ultra nationalistic songs, some of which were laced with very anti Semitic words. But even then very few Jews were seriously concerned, and their general opinion was that the government, like so many others before, would disappear and some other faction would come to power. How wrong they were! In the meantime, life went on.

During the summer, my parents rented a small house in a fishing village located on the Baltic Sea. The village of *Haffkrug* was very close to a famous resort in that area called *Travemuende* (meaning *Mouth of the Trave*), which was filled with big hotels and a gambling casino. The wide beaches there were dotted with *Strandkörbe*, whose literal translation is beach basket; they are actually very comfortable beach chairs made of bamboo or straw, upholstered inside and built with retractable upholstered foot rests. The top of the chair is removable, like the hood of a baby carriage, if more sun was desired.

Our little house faced the sea and was only separated from the beach by a small street winding along the coast. Daddy drove us there--Mutti, Vera, the housemaid, and me--on the first weekend of our vacation. There was lots of excitement, packing everything, favorite dolls, swimsuits, and books. We stayed for the entire school vacation and Daddy came on weekends. On

Margot, Vera, and parents in *Haffkrug*, on the Baltic Sea

the second weekend, he brought Grosspapa Böninger along, and he stayed with us for a week or two. He was so much fun to have around. I can still see him splashing in the water with us, and I can hear him telling stories in the evening.

Every morning, a horse drawn wagon filled with fresh vegetables and fruits slowly made its way along the beach. The man would ring a bell and stop every 50 feet, and all the women lying on the beach, including Mutti, would buy vegetables and fruits for the day. Then our maid would clean and cook them and serve them fresh at the midday meal.

To our great delight, we could pick our own fresh fruits. Raspberries, blueberries, and currants grew wild about a mile from the beach. Vera and I, along with my friend, Lore Baral, whose family had also rented a house there for the summer, would go out with our baskets and pick the delectable berries from the bushes. It was all perfectly safe. Of course, we came home with scratches and mosquito bites, but we didn't mind. When our baskets were full, we would bring them home, and our maid would make jams, fruit juices, and the most delicious pies and cakes.

My greatest pleasure, however, was going out with the fishermen. I had begged them to take me along, and Mutti had given me permission. Around sundown, we went out to set the nets, attaching them to buoys anchored miles offshore. The next morning, just before sunrise, we went out again to pull the nets into the boats. They were full. I remember hanging flounders on clotheslines to dry. We ate some fresh; others were smoked in smoke houses. Fresh, dried, or smoked, these flounders tasted delicious and were served with homemade potato salad for our evening meal. I have never again tasted fish so fresh. For dessert, we sometimes ate a pudding called "Rote Gruetze," a specialty primarily known in the northern part of Germany, something like a fruit Jell-O made completely from scratch with fresh berries as ingredients and served with a homemade vanilla sauce. We also loved cold fruit soup and cold lemon soup. Both were served with little balls of stiffly whipped egg whites.

That summer we enjoyed ourselves without a care in the world. We came home tanned and rested and ready for another school year.

That fall, Mutti had to have what was called "a female operation." Some subjects, of course, were not discussed with children. Later in life, when I was better informed, I figured out that Mutti had had a hysterectomy, although she was extremely young for undergoing that kind of surgery. She was only 36 years old. It might have been the result of a poorly performed abortion. I learned later that Mutti had been pregnant again when Vera was a few years old and that the pregnancy was terminated. I do not know whether this was done on the advice of Mutti's physician or because my parents decided that they did not want any more children. Even as adults, we did not talk about it. There were certain subjects that we just did not discuss. How times have changed.

Mutti's operation was a success, and Daddy was extremely happy. He told both Vera and me that he would buy us a special present and we should tell him what we really wanted. My greatest wish was to have a bicycle. Daddy went with me to a bicycle store and let me chose the bicycle I wanted. I was absolutely elated. Now I felt I was really free and independent; I had my own transportation. After riding around the neighborhood for a while, I started to ride my bicycle to school every day and used it for all my errands and trips to see my friends. I felt free as a bird. My bicycle would take me anywhere I wanted to go. I started to explore the city of Hamburg, and after a while I knew every

Margot and her bicycle in the woods outside Hamburg

neighborhood and every street. Traffic then wasn't what it is today. Very few people owned automobiles, and it was quite safe for a young girl to roam the city on her own. I loved my freedom, and my curiosity took me to every corner of my beautiful hometown of Hamburg.

Of course, owning a bicycle at that time was as common as owning a television is today. Quite a number of my girlfriends in school had bicycles too, and we would make appointments to ride to school together. By that time, we had become rather proficient and could ride our bikes without holding on to the handlebars and could perform other tricks as well. Since the traffic was not heavy, one morning three of us hooked our arms together and peddled down the street showing off our abilities--three bicycles in a row--and obstructing traffic; we had lots of laughs doing it until a policeman spotted us and hauled the three of us into the nearest police station. The charge was obstructing traffic and endangering other people. Our good humor quickly died. First, our parents would be notified, and then there would be punishment. In addition, we would be late for school and be called into the director's office where we would be punished for being late and for our bad behavior.

The other two girls decided that I should ride to school by myself, if the police would let me. This way, I would not be late and could explain to the teacher what had happened. They hoped this would result in less punishment for all of us. They knew our teacher, Mr. Streim, liked me and trusted me, and they thought I could make him see the whole incident in a lighter manner. I also pleaded with the police not to notify our parents. In the end, we were not punished after we promised that we would, in the future, behave more like young ladies and not like circus performers.

Chapter XIII
Youth Groups

In 1933, when I was 13, I joined the Jewish Youth Organization, DJJ. Its full name was *Deutsch-Juedische Jugend* (German-Jewish Youths).

The DJJ was like the Boy Scouts and Girl Scouts, with separate groups for boys and for girls. We wore uniforms of navy blue skirts and green camp shirts with navy blue kerchiefs folded into triangles and tied around our collars. In cooler weather, we wore gray velveteen bomber jackets. Looking back, it seems very odd: I both embarrassed my mother, who thought girls should always be well dressed, and at the same time we looked very much like the young Germans who were part of Hitler's Youth.

We were divided into groups of 10 to 15 boys or girls, mostly of the same age, and each group was led by a young man (never a girl) who was usually a few years older than we were. Older men, usually university students or working men, conducted the meetings and seminars and planned the various activities. Girls in those days were never given leadership positions.

I remember Guenther Friedlaender, a rabbinical student who later became the rabbi of a synagogue in Buenos Aires, Argentina. Even then, I was already strongly opinionated, and I got into violent arguments with Guenther, trying to convince him that my point of view was, of course, better than his.

I met my first serious, steady boyfriend, Helmuth Heineman,

at the DJJ. (He also immigrated to Argentina and settled in Buenos Aires.) When I met Helmuth, he was working at the export firm of Hugo Hartig, and later on he helped me get an apprenticeship with them. Even though he was six years older than I was, we began going steady.

The DJJ met once or twice weekdays in the early evening and on Sabbath afternoons. We discussed current events, Judaism, and, of course, we talked

Helmuth Heineman

about the advances of the Hitler regime, the growing threat to Jews, and what, if anything, could be done about it. We were encouraged to read Hitler's book, *Mein Kampf*, which we discussed at our meetings. There was no doubt that Hitler wanted to eliminate the Jews from Germany.

During the summer months, we went on weekend outings, either by bicycle or by train, and then on walking tours. Martin Buber conducted one of the seminars held in the countryside outside of Hamburg. Dr. Buber, the German-Jewish philosopher, was not only a prolific writer, but a wonderful orator who helped us take pride in our religion and in our rich heritage, even in those difficult times. Dr. Buber, together with Franz Rosenzweig, translated the *Five Books of Moses* into modern German. I was given this translation shortly before I left Germany, and I have cherished it throughout the years.

On other weekends, we would just ride our bicycles into the countryside, enjoy nature, and sleep in tents or in farm houses.

Sometimes, we cooked over camp fires, and once we ate unusual, raw vegetarian food that one farmer offered us.

Since we usually went with a number of other groups from the DJJ, there were always endless pounds of potatoes to peel and vegetables to clean, but we

DJJ members peeling potatoes

always had great fun. After sundown, we would sit around camp fires and sing songs, or somebody would tell stories until we were tired enough to sleep, except when we slept in the straw-covered attic of a farm house and the noise of mice kept us awake all night. As you could imagine, this caused a lot of excitement for us city girls. The attic was divided with a wooden wall, so the girls slept on one side and the boys slept on the other. The only way up or down was by climbing a ladder, which the boys hid from us during the night. It was too high to jump down without breaking our legs, so we had to beg the boys and promise them all kinds of favors before they brought the ladder back.

On Sundays, once or twice a month, we would go with our group for an outing to the countryside around Hamburg. While the north German landscape is flat, it is still very beautiful, and it is

DJJ group with pendant

dotted with a number of small and large lakes. The woods are lovely, filled with old trees. We would either take our bicycles or take a train and then spend the day walking. It now seems strangely ironic that we formed the same kinds of groups as our German counterparts. We even marched in formation in our uniforms, and the leader of our group carried a pennant with the letters "DJJ" on it. Except for the different colors of our uniforms, we looked very much like the groups of Hitler youths marching through the German countryside.

Sometimes, our paths crossed, and this created some unfortunate incidents. They wanted to know who we were, and when they learned that we were a Jewish group, they invariably wanted to start a fight. Somehow, the leader of our group always managed to calm them down and get us safely away. While it gave us a very uncomfortable feeling, it was still the early stages of the Hitler regime and Jews had not yet been stripped of their civil rights.

Some time after joining the DJJ, I also became a member of their affiliated sports club, called *Schild* (Shield). I started in their track and field team and was part of their relay running group. I liked the running and jumping competitions and I loved being outdoors. When I was about 15, I joined the women's field hockey team. They started me on the 3rd team and later advanced me to the 2nd team. Because I was a fast runner, my position was right half back.

My life became very busy with all of these extracurricular activities, but there was one strict rule in our house: we all had to be home for the evening meal on weekdays, for the Sabbath meal on Friday nights, and for the main meal on Saturdays and Sundays. We were never excused from the Sunday midday meal, even if there was an important event on the sports field. Despite the impending troubles, these years and my membership in the DJJ left me with wonderful memories and with the utmost respect for my family and for my family's traditions.

Chapter XIV

The English Correspondent

I always thought I would become an attorney. I had an inquisitive mind; I liked to study; and I was good at debating. In any case, everyone else assumed that after finishing high school I would study law. However, at the age of 15, after reading Hitler's opinions and becoming well-informed about politics and the future of Jews in Germany, I knew I would not have the chance to pursue my dream career in my homeland. I knew that sooner or later my family and I would have to emigrate and that I would have to be able to support myself and, perhaps, even help my parents.

Hitler's *Mein Kampf*, a passionate confabulation of his life story and his political opinions, was scary reading to a young Jewish girl. The book was published in 1925, and by the time I was fifteen, ten years later, Hitler had amassed a huge following, and his ideology was spreading. Anti-Semitic regulations would soon follow. Hitler's views about the Jews were terrifying to me.

Many of my father's friends, indeed many German Jews, thought Hitler would eventually be voted out of office or overthrown, but I didn't. I thought he was already too well entrenched. I had a terrible foreboding about it. I was more than uneasy and saw the fate of any Jewish merchant or any Jewish business in jeopardy. How would I, a young Jewish girl trying to get ahead in her career, fare under these circumstances?

I could in no way imagine my life the same way my parents and grandparents saw theirs. I was nervous. I felt the lives of those I loved to be vulnerable. And although I could never imagine the horrors that would ensue, I sensed that Hitler would not stop. Under these circumstances, how could I go forward with my studies?

Therefore, in the summer of 1935, at the start of the summer vacation, I decided to quit school and become an apprentice in a commercial enterprise in order to learn the skills necessary to become a secretary. I had learned English and French in school and was rather good in German composition and very good in spelling and excellent in every kind of mathematics.

I had no difficulty leaving school because I'd already completed the required eight years of education. Apprentices, however, were required to go to trade school a few evenings during the week, and I started taking classes at the State School for Office Employees. I learned bookkeeping and office procedures, as well as how to calculate prices. I also enrolled in a private business school, *Handelschuhle R. Feldt*, where I learned German and English stenography and touch-typing.

My official apprenticeship began in July of 1935 with the firm of *Treetex G.M.B.H.*, a subsidiary of *Hugo Hartig*, a well established international trading company founded by a Jewish man named Hugo Hartig. The owner at that time was Charles Hartig, the son of the founder.

In 1935, at least for the time being, a Jewish firm was still able to conduct normal business in Germany, even business with government agencies, even road construction and the building trade.

Treetex imported pressed wood sheets from Sweden. This product was used primarily in road construction and as insulating material in new buildings. For road construction, the boards were laid down crosswise into the roadbed every hundred yards to prevent the asphalt from splitting during rapid or severe changes in the weather.

My job turned out to be very interesting. I was learning office procedures, but, in reality, I became a junior secretary. I took dictation in shorthand and typed letters, and I did the filing and whatever else was required of me. I felt quite grown-up and in most cases I was treated as an equal.

There was only one office duty, however, that still marked me as an apprentice. It was the custom every morning to have a so-called "second breakfast." Somebody would come around with a wagon offering sandwiches and light pastries. The female underlings--and I was certainly one of them--had to prepare tea in large earthenware pitchers and personally serve the executives in their private offices.

One morning, I found myself serving tea in Charles Hartig's office. He was a nice looking man, in his forties, and all the young girls, including me, had a crush on him. That was the only good part about serving the tea!

I remember that Mr. Hartig looked up at me, scrutinized my appearance and clothing, and said, "Fräulein Schragenheim, I see you have lint all over your dress. The next time you come to my office, please make sure you brush your dress properly before entering my office."

I was mortified. My face flushed, and I backed out of the office crushed and ashamed. I wished the ground would open up in front of me. Alone, I looked down at my very well-tailored, navy blue dress. Yes, there was some lint and tiny bits of paper scraps on the front. I was learning the embarrassing way that in the business world appearances matter.

My immediate boss, Mr. Schwarzchild, was the head of the *Treetex* division. It was whispered he was having an affair with his secretary. He was very pleasant, but sometimes had a strange way of expressing himself.

Vice President of Personnel, Margot, Mr. Schwarzschild (in white shirt), and his two secretaries, 1936

But pretty soon I became part of the inner circle. I still have pictures of a group of us sunning ourselves during lunch hour on one of the fishing boats anchored just a short walk from our office building. There we were, Mr. Schwarzschild and his secretary, the senior vice president in charge of personnel, and two other secretaries from our department. I'd been accepted among them. I even dated a few of the young men who worked for the firm, but nothing serious came from it.

Once a year during the summer, Charles Hartig gave a party for all his employees on his large estate in the outskirts of Hamburg. It was a grand affair, with long tables set up in his garden and wonderful food served by the finest caterers. It was a time for all the young employees to feel valued. From people like Mr. Hartig, I learned how important it is to treat employees well, to keep up morale, and to reward people for good service.

Charles Hartig's summer party on his estate outside of Hamburg, 1936

My apprenticeship finished at the end of June 1937, and I was pleased when the firm offered me a secretarial job. However, my instinct told me I would be forced to leave Germany soon, and I thought I needed to plan more carefully and not just jump at the first job that came around.

I knew I needed to perfect my English skills--in both dictation and in writing--so against everyone's opinion that I was making a big mistake, I declined their offer. I struck out on my own and started answering ads in the *Hamburger Fremdenblatt*. I was relieved when I got a job interview for the position of English Correspondent with the firm of *J. Jacobi*.

I interviewed with the head of the firm, Mr. Weizsenstein, a man in his forties, not particularly good-looking but impeccably dressed.

He spoke German with a pronounced foreign accent. I later learned he was born in Hungary. During the interview, I recited all my credentials to Mr. Weizsenstein, including my English lessons, my typing and stenography skills, and I said, "I believe I am capable of fulfilling the position." I told him I had been an apprentice at *Hugo Hartig* for the past two years, and I showed him my letter of recommendation.

"This all sounds very good, Fräulein Schragenheim," he answered me, smiling, "but now let's see how well you can really do all the things you just described?"

Staring him straight in the eyes and returning his smile, I said quite convincingly and rather cockily, "I am sure I will do a good job, and you will definitely be satisfied."

I left without knowing whether or not I got the job, but a few days later I received a postcard in the mail advising me that I had been hired and would start on July 1, 1937. Apparently, I made a good impression. My monthly salary was 120.00 Deutsche Marks. It was quite an improvement over my measly salary of 40.00 Marks as an apprentice!

J. Jacobi & Co. were exporters of general merchandise, primarily with East Asian countries. I was assigned to a small department with its own office, where three young men oversaw business with China. The correspondence was mostly in English, and I was the only secretary for the three of them.

I will never forget the first day in my new position and the first letter dictated to me. It was a very long, detailed letter in English. The young man (whose name I have long forgotten) asked me to read my steno notes back to him. I stumbled over some of the words that I had not understood properly, but he was very kind and patient and suggested that I write the difficult words in longhand. Then I started typing the letter, and while I was usually a fast typist I was incredibly slow with this first try because I wasn't always sure of my spelling and I was embarrassed to ask for a dictionary. I could feel everyone's eyes on the back of my head, watching me plod through my first assignment, starting over several times.

When the draft was finally finished, it still contained many errors, but the young man was very understanding. He made the corrections and let me re-type the letter. I still gratefully remember the patience these three men showed me, guiding me along, and I eventually developed into the competent secretary they needed. I also learned an incredible amount of English in the process, which helped me enormously later in my life.

One day, after only working there a few weeks, I was called in to take dictation from the big boss, Mr. Weizsenstein. His private secretary had not come to work, and I was the only one available who could take English dictation. I was a nervous wreck. While I had improved during the few weeks I had worked there, I was far from perfect. I didn't think I was up to the job.

After a perfunctory greeting, we got on with the letter writing. My knees were knocking. He was hard enough to understand in German with his Hungarian accent, and his English was even worse. He also had the confounding habit of looking out the window when he spoke so that only his back was turned to me, and he had a tendency to mumble. More than a few times, I had to ask him to repeat what he'd said. I was greatly relieved when we finished, but then my problems began anew. I had, of course, missed a few words here and there, so I made a rough draft and ran back to my own department where my co-workers came to my rescue and helped me fix my mistakes. Mr. Weizsenstein would never know what a toll that single business letter took on Fräulein Schragenheim.

Generally, I enjoyed working at *J. Jacobi & Co.* The office was at #10 *Neuerwall* in a multi-story office building, a prestigious address, just a few steps from the famous shopping street, *Jungfernstieg*.

Instead of elevators, this building had a contraption called a "Patanosta," a series of cabinets, which were open in front and were raised and lowered with heavy iron chains that slid over the roof top. They moved very slowly, and anyone could step on and off on any floor without difficulty.

This peculiar "Patanosta" also became a lovers' rendezvous. Young men and women working in the building would make appointments to meet, and, at the unoccupied top floor where the cars slowed down and made their turn downward again, the young lovers would exchange their kisses.

I was in awe of Helga Cohn, the boss' private secretary. She was nine or ten years my senior and I found her very sophisticated. She was attractive, of medium height, and slim. She had beautiful blonde hair and was always well dressed. Gossip had it that she was the boss's girlfriend. Many years later, after both of us were married, we met accidentally in New York. It turned out that our husbands had been good friends in Ber-

The staff of J. Jacobi on the roof of *Neuer Wall* 10 during a lunch break, Hamburg, 1937

lin, and the two men were happy to be reunited through us. After that, the four of us spent wonderful times together, and my husband and I had the pleasure of seeing their only daughter grow up. Helga's husband, Walter, died comparatively young, but Helga and I remained friends to the end of her days.

Although the gossip that Helga Cohn had been Mr. Weizsenstein's girlfriend had been true, the affair ended and both married other people.

All in all, I was treated well, yet my job with *J. Jacobi* lasted only three months. Japan invaded parts of China, and trading was halted and our department was closed. They wrote me a very nice letter of recommendation, which also reads as a sad commentary on those difficult times:

"Margot Schragenheim, born August 24, 1920, worked for us from July 1 to September 30, 1937, as a German and English Correspondent. We were satisfied with her achievements. Unfortunately, we have to dismiss her as well as a few of the other personnel who were hired recently due to conditions in the Far East. This is the only reason we had to let Miss Schragenheim go."

I am still very proud that within three months I had merited this wonderful recommendation.

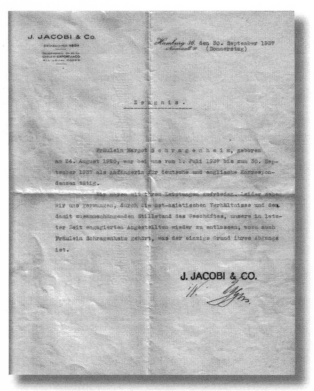

The Letter of Recommendation
from J. Jacobi & Co.

Chapter XV

My First Great Love

Hans Heinrich was 18 years old, slim with straight, brown hair which he parted neatly on the right side. His deeply set eyes were sparkling gray. He was of medium height, just a few inches taller than I was, and had a somewhat serious air about him, but when he smiled his face lit up and his good looks became more pronounced.

Hans Heinrich at age 18

We met on the hockey field. He played goalie for the men's team, and when he asked me to have coffee with him at the snack bar, I immediately said yes.

He told me that he had just graduated from the *Gymnasium* and was working at an international trading firm. He was being groomed there before entering his father's business, which

Margot and Hans Heinrich on the hockey field, 1937

he was supposed to take over. The year was 1935 and looking back, it seems quite strange that a successful and intelligent businessman was not aware that under Hitler's regime there would be no future in Germany for a business owned and run by a Jew. But he was not the only one. Many of my parents' friends and relatives at that time still thought that Hitler and his gang would not last. They felt that Germans would eventually elect a different government and that Germany would go back to being a democratic country as it was before Hitler came to power. They just could not believe that as loyal German citizens--indeed, many had fought in the First World War--they would not be able to live peacefully in their beloved country.

"Where do you live?" Hans Heinrich asked me as we finished our coffee.

"*St. Benedictstrasse 24,*" I replied.

"What a coincidence," he said. "I live just around the corner. Why don't we ride home together?"

We did, talking all the way.

He told me that his father was an exporter who dealt primarily with Central and South American countries. His father was in his sixties and was looking forward to turning over his very successful business to his only son. His son-in-law, who was married to his oldest daughter, was a rich gentleman farmer who lived on a large estate outside of Hamburg and had no interest in the business. His second daughter, Miggi, who was two years older than Hans Heinrich, was engaged to be married to a very attractive and charming man who had just finished his studies in medicine. That left Hans Heinrich as heir apparent, a role he really did not relish. "I really want to become an auto racer," he told me, "but I know my father will never let me do that."

Hans Heinrich's father was a strong, domineering man, and eventually the son would bend to his father's wishes. After we went home together on our bicycles a few times, Hans Heinrich asked me for a date. At first, I didn't know whether to accept. He was pleasant enough, but I was not that attracted to him. I had been going out with a number of older boys and I thought an 18-year-old might actually be too young and immature for me. I had just turned 16, but I thought of myself as very grown up, so much so that I said to my best girlfriend, "I don't know wheth-

Margot at age 16

er I want to go out with Hans Heinrich. After all, I don't want to rob the cradle." Looking back on that episode, I can only wonder, "What was I thinking?"

But Hans Heinrich, who apparently was very attracted to me, used all of his charm until I finally accepted his invitation to go dancing with him. The place he chose was very romantic. It was summer and he selected an outdoor restaurant in a park-like setting. The restaurant, *Planten and Blomen*, which in the Low German dialect means *Plants and Flowers*, was, indeed, filled with many beautiful plants and flowers and the outdoor park was interwoven with waterways and fountains covered with water lilies. Small tables and comfortable chairs were placed around a rather large dance floor, and the tables and the surrounding trees were all illuminated.

Hans Heinrich turned out to be a wonderful host. He knew just what to order, and money seemed to be no object. In addition, he was a fabulous dancer. We had a great time on that first date. He was charming and solicitous. We talked about music and art and about his love of cars. We gossiped and shared secrets. We danced between courses and after coffee, until I finally said, "I think you'd better take me home now."

He later taught me how to dance the tango in front of the mirror in his room. I must have learned well because many years later my old school friend, Uschi, remarked, "To see you and Hans Heinrich put down a tango was always a pleasure to watch." He also had a number of interests outside of sports and cars. He loved music and he loved art. We talked about the various operas, concerts, and plays we attended. Hamburg had a lot to offer: a very good opera house and a variety of great theaters, where they performed classical pieces, serious dramas, comedies, and operettas. We enjoyed excellent concerts and variety shows and good museums, and Hans Heinrich and I were both brought up to appreciate culture, good music, fine art, excellent food, and an elegant atmosphere. It turns out that I really began to like him, and each time he took me home and asked me for another date, I was quite happy to say "Yes."

One date followed another, a few kisses made us feel closer to each other, and after a while we were "going steady." We went to restaurants and nightclubs and Sunday afternoon tea dances. Because we were still very young, a few clubs would not let us in, but we always laughed about it and usually found another place where we could go. We spent New Year's 1937 together, Hans Heinrich in tuxedo, and I in a black chiffon evening gown. We felt so grown up. We lived and worked close to each other, and we would try to ride together to and from work. Sometimes, we met for lunch. When there were no hockey games or training sessions on a Sunday, we would ride our bicycles into the beautiful countryside. Hamburg was surrounded by woods and lakes and if the weather was good (not always the case in Hamburg and surroundings), it was lovely to be out of the city. On one of these outings, we stopped for a picnic at a beautifully secluded spot on a lake. There wasn't a soul around and we decided to go skinny dipping. We were both good swimmers and had great fun exploring the secluded lake. When we came out of the water and saw each other standing there naked, nature took over and we made love for the first time. We were both virgins, but it did not matter. Nature seems to have a way of guiding two young people who are in love.

Coming home, I felt somewhat guilty but knew I should not confide in anybody, and I didn't. Of course, the two of us now became even closer, but a place to be alone together was hard to come by. The weather was not always conducive, and fall was fast approaching.

One Saturday night, we went for dinner and dancing in the country. Since we were properly dressed, we went by suburban train instead of by bicycle. After a wonderful dinner and lots of dancing, we headed back toward the train station, where we found a bench in a secluded spot. Since we knew the train would not come for another 45 minutes, we decided that this would be a good spot, even if it was a little uncomfortable, to try our love making again. Unfortunately, we became so involved that we missed the train. "What now?" I asked. It was around midnight and we were in a little village in the countryside. "How can we get home?" We walked around, found an open garage, and Hans Heinrich persuaded the owner to drive us home. He always had quite a lot of money on him. I finally sneaked into our apartment extremely late and made absolutely sure not to wake my parents. The consequences would have been horrible.

One fine day, however, disaster really did strike. Hans Heinrich's parents were away on business in South America, and his grandmother, who lived with them, was taking her afternoon nap in her upstairs bedroom. It was a quiet Sunday and the servants were out of the house. What a perfect opportunity to again try our love making. There was a small den next to the entrance hall of the villa, which we thought was far enough away from Hans Heinrich's grandmother's bedroom upstairs; she must have heard us, however, and before we knew it we were discovered.

The next day, the grandmother paid my mother a visit. "Frau Schragenheim," she explained to my mother, "my daughter and son-in-law are in South America and I am supposed to be in charge, but my grandchildren make life difficult for me! My granddaughter, Miggi, and her fiancé are always giving boisterous parties when their parents are away." It was true and at these parties there were always young people drinking, smoking, dancing, and necking; grandmother could hardly cope with this. "Miggi's fiancé, who is a medical intern, plays all kinds of jazz music for these people," Hans Heinrich's grandmother told my mother, "and they dance wildly until odd hours of the night. Then yesterday," she continued, "I found my grandson and your daughter making love in our den. Please, Frau Schragenheim, help me, help me by stopping it. Please, please do something." She was in despair. It really was too much for her, and she felt my mother should know what was going on and should stop it.

When I came home that evening, all hell broke loose. Mutti had told Daddy and I was confronted and had to tell them the truth, which I did. I was told that I could never see Hans Heinrich again and I was not allowed to go out for many, many months. Naturally, I cried and screamed at my parents, telling them how cruel they were, that they had no understanding of what it was like to be young, that these were modern times, that I loved this boy, Hans Heinrich, and that they were ruining, literally ruining, my life. I also probably said all the other things teenagers tell their parents when they have a fight.

While Hans Heinrich and I still saw each other when we went to work, my father suspected this and followed us in his car. When I came home in the evening, my dear father, who was usually so mild mannered, laid down the law. Hans Heinrich, however, came to see my parents and told them how much he loved me and that he really wanted to marry me as soon as he could support a wife.

My parents felt he was sincere, and my father did what any father would do: he made an appointment with Hans Heinrich's father and told him the whole story. My father told Mr. Knobloch that even though Hans Heinrich and I were very young (by then, I was 17 and he was 19), we should go ahead and get married. If both fathers helped financially, my father explained, it could be managed easily until we were able to stand on our own feet. Hans Heinrich's father refused outright. His son was much too young to take on such a responsibility, he said to my father, and he would not agree to such an arrangement, not now, not ever. The truth is I wasn't aware of this conversation until 55 years later when I met Hans Heinrich again and he told me the story.

Hans Heinrich, without telling me any of this at the time, wanted to show me that he was completely sincere and that he really wanted to marry me. He knew our parents objected, and I was forbidden to see him altogether, so he suggested we secretly get engaged, which we did. On September 29, 1937, we exchanged gold engagement rings. In Germany at that time, plain gold wedding bands were exchanged at the engagement, and the rings were worn on the left ring fingers. On the wedding day, the rings were exchanged again and they were placed on the right ring fingers. I still have the ring, which is engraved with Hans Heinrich's initials and the date of the engagement. We managed to see each other secretly, but, of course, not as often as before. His sister, Miggi, and Fritz got married. Hans Heinrich was the best man, and he was terribly upset because he was not allowed to invite me to the wedding. Miggi and I also became very good friends. She and Fritz immigrated to New York, and when I lived in New York we saw quite a bit of each other and enjoyed each other's company.

Early in 1938, Hans Heinrich's parents left again on a business trip to South America and never came back to Hamburg. By then, they had realized that there was no future for Jews in Germany, and

I suppose his father made financial arrangements with his business connections to preserve as much of his money outside of Germany as possible. Hans Heinrich followed them in early March of 1938. We promised each other that we would do everything we could to be together again. We loved each other and we hoped that in spite of all the obstacles we would find a way to get married. As a farewell present, Hans Heinrich gave me a German translation of the Five Books of Moses. This translation was written by the famous Martin Buber in collaboration with the equally renowned Franz Rosenzweig. Hans Heinrich's dedication in the book reads as follows:

To my beloved little girl in support and admiration and as a re-membrance from your friend and hopefully future husband.

–Hans Heinrich

We corresponded. In October of that year, I left for the United States, and we wrote each other long, sad love letters. I even tried to become a stewardess on ships sailing to South America, but I could not get those jobs because I was not an American citizen. Hans Heinrich tried to come to America as a stowaway, but he did not succeed. Life went on and one day I wrote to him that I had found a new boyfriend. I told him that I still loved him and hoped we could plan a life together in the future. This letter was never answered.

Many years later, after I had been married for more than 25 years, I did receive a letter from Hans Heinrich. He had found my address through roundabout ways. He and his wife were coming to New York, and they wanted to get together with us. We met in the lobby of the Statler Hotel. He had changed little. I took them to our apartment, served drinks and dinner, and my husband Henry and I spent a delightful evening with them. Elenita, Hans Heinrich's wife who spoke English fluently, told me that Hans Heinrich had never forgotten me, that he had pictures of me in his house, and that he talked about me all the time. She was very excited to

Photo of Margot in the home of Hans Heinrich

meet me. She and Hans Heinrich seemed very happy, even though her background was entirely different from his. She was a Catholic girl who was born in Argentina and raised by nuns. They had two children, who were both brought up as Catholics: a daughter, Inge, and a son, Rolf (typical German names to which she obviously did not object). My Henry enjoyed their company, too; he found Hans Heinrich intelligent, charming, and good-looking, and he said he could understand that I had once loved him. It was an enjoyable evening for all of us, and from then on we stayed in touch.

In 1994, I received the strangest letter written in English from Hans Heinrich's wife, asking me if I could accompany him to Germany and help him straighten out his somewhat tangled affairs there. After all, I spoke German, and, as I was a very good business woman, she felt I could help Hans Heinrich better than anybody else, and together we would obtain the best results. I declined but put Hans Heinrich in touch with a friend living in West Germany. Because of this, Hans Heinrich and I communicated a lot, and he told me that after he settled matters in Germany he wanted to visit me on his way back to South America. He did. We spent a few very enjoyable days together, talked about old times and about our current lives. Of course, we had lived such entirely different lives in different parts of the world; we were 55 years older and our views and ideas had very much changed. We had sex but it wasn't great. Perhaps it had never been! We really cannot return to the time when we were young, and it isn't possible to pick up where we left off. At least, wonderful memories remain.

We met again in December 1999, in Buenos Aires. I'd been a widow for six years by then, and my sister, brother-in-law, and I had booked a cruise on the "Crystal Harmony" to celebrate the Millennium New Year's Eve on board the ship in the bay of Rio de Janeiro. Hans Heinrich was living in Montevideo, Uruguay, which is just a ferry ride across from Buenos Aires. I had written to him that I would love to see him again.

"Perhaps you and Elenita could join us for a few days in Buenos Aires," I wrote. I gave him the dates and the hotel. Sure enough, he showed up, but without Elenita. He was there at lunchtime on the day we arrived. Like all of us, he, too, had gotten older. But he'd changed in other ways, too. While he had always been an impeccable dresser, his clothes now looked worn and old-fashioned, and his whole demeanor was somewhat subdued. We sat in the lobby of the hotel, and we talked about our lives, about politics, about family, and about friends. Then he said, "Can I see your hotel room?" Since I really didn't feel like having sex with him, I replied, "Hans Heinrich, don't you think we are getting a little too old for this?" He did not answer, and we still managed to have a good time with Vera and her husband, Louis.

We went to a show in Buenos Aires, we toured the opera house, and we had lunches and dinners together. But every now and then, there were little remarks laced with sexual connotations. Our ship was anchored in Buenos Aires for two days, and the day we were set to sail I asked Hans Heinrich to come to breakfast or lunch. He never showed up. I called the hotel where he was staying and was told that he had checked out. I was hurt and upset, and I wrote him a letter saying, "I really had been looking forward to seeing you to reminisce about good old times and to catch up on our lives. I thought we were having a good time by seeing all the wonderful things Buenos Aires has to offer. Is sex really that important for elderly people who have not seen each other in a long time and live different lives? How could you leave without even saying good bye and thanking me for my hospitality?"

I found his reply when I got home. He was disappointed in me, he wrote in his letter, and while he had loved me all his life I now made it possible for him to forget me. So here ends the story of my first great love.

Chapter XVI
We Move Again

D addy's wholesale tobacco business deteriorated for a variety of reasons. Manufacturers raised their prices and Daddy's profits, therefore, became smaller and smaller, especially on the inexpensive cigarettes. Finally, the producers began selling the cheaper brands directly to the retailers, cutting out wholesalers entirely. Hitler had by now been in power for a few years, and anti-Semitism was growing fast in Germany. Daddy had already lost some important accounts because he was Jewish, and he began to sense that even some of his oldest and most valuable customers, even people he thought were friends, were becoming reluctant to buy from a Jew.

In 1937, Daddy decided to sell the business. Another wholesaler, a competitor with whom he was friendly, offered to buy him out. This man felt that even with the loss of the cheaper brands, the combined roster of customers of the two firms would make it possible to continue operating a successful wholesale business. Of course, he was able to buy the business at a depressed price, but in return he offered Daddy a job at a decent salary. He did this even though he knew that it was not advisable to have a Jew in his employ. He obviously was a sensitive man who understood how devastating it would have been for Daddy, at the age of 40, to both lose his business and to be without any work at all.

My father and mother now wanted to move out of the neighborhood where we had owned the business. They decided on *Harvestehude*, a lovely neighborhood where many streets bordered the Alster River. *St. Benedictstrasse* had a number of villas (single-family homes) or two-story homes, which looked very much like converted villas. We moved into a cheery apartment at *St. Benedictstrasse 24*, on the first floor facing a tree-lined street and we settled very happily into the new neighborhood. A number of my friends were living nearby, and I very much liked how close we were to the Alster River. At the end of our street was a little bridge that went over a tributary of the Alster. We liked to congregate at the boathouse where many of the boys in our crowd kept their boats. In spite of what was going on around us, we were very carefree. We laughed and sang and flirted the way teenagers do.

Some of the boys had small sailboats, and since the Alster was as wide as a lake it was ideal for sailing as long as there was a little wind. I was thrilled to sail in the boats or row with the boys in their beautiful canoes decorated with many colorful pillows.

We had great fun on the canoes; we ate and drank and listened to music on a portable record player. When two boys and two girls would go out, the boys would paddle the boat and the girls would recline on the soft pillows and listen to the music. If we were just two of us, one boy and one girl, both of us would paddle until we found an idyllic spot--and there were plenty--especially in the tributaries of the Alster. We would talk, listen to music, or perhaps even engage in a little smooching.

Some evenings if we really wanted to have fun, a few of us would paddle to the *Uhlenhorster Faehrhaus*, an elegant res-

Margot smoking a pipe in a canoe on the Alster River, 1938

taurant in a white, old-fashioned building located at the edge of the Alster in a section called *Uhlenhorst*, which was opposite to *Harvestehude*. The restaurant had a large outdoor patio and on nice summer evenings it was set up for outdoor dining. There was a dance floor in the center and a small band played delightful music. Somehow, the boys managed to tie up the boats on the side of the patio and we would climb out and start dancing until we were chased away by the Maitre d'. They were usually fairly tolerant with us and we would manage to get in at least one or two dances. On Wednesday evenings, there were fireworks on the dock and we would line up our boats to watch the wonderful display.

The *Uhlenhorster Faehrhaus*, Hamburg, 1938

Opposite the *Uhlenhorster Faehrhaus* on the *Harvestehude* side was a small wooden shack, with a pier on the Alster. It was called "Tante Lo" (Aunt Lo), and while they only served ice cream and soft drinks my friends and I made a real club out of it. We took our record players off the boats, played music, and danced. At some tables, the problems of the world were discussed, while other kids just acted silly. Thinking back, it seems incredible that in 1937, with the Nazi regime already in power for four years, we still enjoyed ourselves so much and had such a good time like youngsters would growing up under more normal circumstances. What a pleasure it was to be young and without a care in the world.

Chapter XVII
The Temple

Despite our Orthodox grandparents' objections, my parents decided to join a more liberal synagogue. Our new apartment was much closer to this temple on *Oberstrasse*. Besides, our parents felt more comfortable in the modern environment and they liked the services the temple offered. Vera and I were also pleased with the decision, since by that time many of our friends attended the newer temple on *Oberstrasse* and not the larger Orthodox synagogue on *Bornplatz*.

The temple building was very modern: square with a light stone wall as its façade and wide steps that led up to the handsome bronze doors. The sanctum had dark, wooden benches. But although it was a liberal synagogue and featured an organ and choir, men and women still sat separately. The women sat upstairs and the men sat downstairs. Daddy sat on the right side downstairs, and Mutti, Vera, and I sat on the left side upstairs; that way, we could see one another, and sometimes we communicated by sign language.

The service was beautiful and very dignified. Our beloved Rabbi Italiener was a knowledgeable, interesting speaker,

The bima in the
Oberstrasse Temple

and our cantor had an impressive voice. The mixed choir was excellent, and some of the singers were from the Hamburg Opera. The *Oberstrasse* Temple's services were shorter than the ones at the Orthodox synagogue; they were mostly in Hebrew and there were no responsive readings. The only similar service that I have ever participated in was years later at Congregation *Habonim*, in New York. The synagogue was founded by German Jews, and the rabbi and the cantor were from Germany as well. I joined Congregation Habonim about a year after arriving in America, and it almost felt as if I were back at my temple in Hamburg.

Now that my family and I were within walking distance of the temple it made it easier to attend services. I especially loved going on Friday nights because it was also a way to meet both my girlfriends and boyfriends. And we usually went for long walks afterwards.

PART III

Chapter XVIII
The Meyers and Starting Life in America

I approached a small wooden house on a busy commercial street in Irvington, New Jersey. It was October 1938. I had arrived in New York Harbor just a few hours earlier, and now after my journey by car under the Hudson River I walked eagerly toward the front porch of my new home. The door opened and there was Bertha Meyer waiting for me.

Bertha Meyer was a small, inherently shy woman--sallow, wrinkle-faced with graying hair--but on that day she tried her best to brighten her mood; she knew instinctively how important it was to make me feel at home, and she did. She welcomed me in German, and even though I was a complete stranger she enveloped me in a big hug and gave me a warm kiss.

The men lugged my steamer trunk upstairs into my room. It was a cheerful room with white curtains through which I could see a tree whose leaves were re-

Charles and Bertha Meyer in front of their home in Irvington, NJ, 1938

splendent in fall colors. The room had a single bed, a chest of drawers, and a table with two chairs against the window. I longed to get settled in.

Even though it was the 23rd of October, it was warm, and I quickly changed out of my traveling clothes, a beautifully fitted gray-blue tweed coat with a matching skirt and a white silk blouse, which were much more suited for the chilly, damp Hamburg autumns than this lovely American Indian Summer day. Then I went downstairs to get to know the Meyers.

All the meals in the Meyers' home were served on a wooden table in the kitchen, which stood with its narrow end against a wall. I hope I never showed my disappointment or said anything inappropriate, but never in the 18 years that I lived in Hamburg or during any visits to relatives or friends, for that matter, had I ever eaten in a kitchen. I would have to get used to this and to many other new American customs.

It sounds snobbish today, I know, but only maids ate in the kitchen at any of the homes I had been in. I reminded myself that this was a very different country with very different habits and that my newly found relatives were very poor; I told myself I'd better make the best of it.

Aunt Bertha cooked very plain food, a soup and meat with potatoes and vegetables. Plain or fancy, good or bad, it didn't matter. I was a hungry teenager who had been brought up to eat everything that was on the table. And I did. We usually had cookies or pie for dessert, sometimes with vanilla ice cream. I must say that I fell in love immediately with American ice cream. It was so much richer than the ice cream in Germany.

Although I was certainly appreciative, my life in the Meyers' household was not very exciting. Almost every night after helping clean up, we would sit at the kitchen table and play yet another game of Pinochle. Over the cards, the Meyers would ask me questions about my parents and my sister--they did not know them--and about the rest of the family they knew in Germany.

Mostly, they would ask about Grosspapa Böninger, who was Aunt Bertha's brother. As far as I could tell, the Meyers did not have any intellectual interests, nor did they seem to have any close friends. Neither did they go out or venture into New York City, which was really not that far from Irvington. The extent of their social life seemed to revolve around getting together with their son and daughter-in-law on weekends.

Charles and Bertha Meyer and their son, Charlie, and his wife, Ruth

Although their house was on one of the main streets--and across from a gas station--Irvington was still a small town and quite a change for me. Looking back, I realize how really young I was in 1938--eighteen--but somehow I had always been keenly aware that I was from a sophisticated European city.

The Meyers did offer me some interesting advice. Uncle Charlie was proud to be an American with American habits. "Don't save on bus fare," he would tell me. "You Europeans are great savers, but very often it does not make sense. For some reason, you'd rather walk than take a bus which costs only five cents, and then you end up spending your money on heels and soles for your shoes!" The man had a point.

Charles Meyer and his son, Charlie, were partners in a small house painting business. Charlie's wife was pregnant and money

Charles Meyer & Sons
business card

was tight. After just a few days, I was informed that my Uncle Charles had found a job for me in a factory just a short walking distance from their home. I could stay with them, but they expected me to pay for room and board.

Actually, I liked the idea of going to work. I would have preferred an office job where my skills would have helped me advance, but this was 1938 and jobs were still very hard to find. Industry and business continued to struggle with the after effects of the Great Depression. I was told that I should be glad to find any work at all, being such a newcomer to the country and not yet fluent in the English language. The next day, Uncle Charles took me to meet the foreman of the factory.

He was a big, formidable-looking man, and he explained that the factory produced metal caps for the tops of the corks on wine bottles. I knew exactly what they looked like on wine bottles, but I had never seen how they were manufactured and shipped. They came in different colors and were stamped out round, then embossed with the winery's logo and name, and then another machine would shape them into cylinders. These cylinders were brought into the packing room where I would work. My job was to take the cylinders and place them on the tops of the corks. Somebody else would wrap them, and they would then be boxed and shipped to the wineries. I was paid the minimum wage, which in 1938 was 25 cents per hour.

The work week was 44 hours: eight hours Monday through Friday and four hours on Saturday. My total weekly pay was $11.00; at that time, social security and income tax were not deducted. It sounds incredible now, but back then I felt I had a pretty good deal.

If I gave the Meyers half of my salary for room and board, I would still have the huge sum of $5.50 per week for movies, ice cream, the occasional visit to the beauty parlor, or for anything else I wanted. I started work immediately.

A number of other girls also stood at the long wooden tables doing the same job I did. The girls, most with dark, curly hair and big, brown eyes, looked like many of my Jewish schoolmates in Germany, only these girls in the factory in Irvington, New Jersey wore crosses on chains around their necks. They were all very nice to me and helped me with my English and explained things to me that I could not understand. After a few days, I asked the girls whether they were Jewish, and if so why in the world were they wearing crosses around their necks? They looked at me like I was crazy and started laughing. They said that they were Italian Catholics and that wearing a cross was very much the thing to do. Yes, indeed, I had much to learn about America; after all, I was still very much the new immigrant.

The weather had been glorious when I arrived on October 23rd, and it stayed that way for a while, but about two weeks later, on November 6th to be exact, it snowed. I woke to find everything covered in white, about eight inches on the ground. I was glad I had brought my beautiful, fur-trimmed, knee-high boots from Germany, and I put them on for my walk to work. I had hardly walked half a block when a woman stopped and asked, "Where in the world did you get those wonderful boots? I can't find any like them anywhere. I can only find the short ones and with snow like this my feet get wet. Where did you buy them? I would like to get a pair."

"It might be a little far for you to go," I said, smiling at her. "I just came over from Germany and brought them with me." She was disappointed, but it was true. At that time, high boots were neither made in nor imported to America.

My job at the bottle factory lasted only a few weeks. Apparently, they had only needed me as extra help for the Christmas season. Uncle Charles, who knew quite a few people through his painting business, tried his best to find me another job in or around Irvington, but nothing turned up.

Chapter XIX
The Housemaid

With the lack of available factory and office jobs, many girls found that the only way they could support themselves was as sleep-in household help. Therefore, I. too, decided to look for a job as a sleep-in housemaid. At that time, a great number of middle-income families hired full time household help, which they could easily afford since free room and board were part of the salary. Even the meager wages were attractive to me. Many refugees and immigrants found this the only way to have both shelter and food and at least some pocket money.

I found a job with a young Jewish couple in Newark, New Jersey. After two busses from Irvington, I surprisingly found their house with ease. It was located in a predominantly middle-class Jewish neighborhood. The couple greeted me in their rather large ground floor apartment. The husband was a doctor who had his office at home. The wife was a teacher. I was hired at $25.00 a month. I had to clean the whole apartment, including the doctor's office, cook three meals for the couple, and cook dinner for frequent dinner parties. I also had to answer the doctor's phone calls and take messages. Believe it or not, that was the hardest part for me because while I could speak English quite well by then, I often had trouble understanding the people speaking on the telephone. While the doctor and his wife were very pleasant, they were not particularly friendly or caring. I was assigned a terribly depressing, windowless room under a staircase, probably just a converted closet. There was a bed, a dresser, a chair, and a bare bulb hanging from the ceiling. But I had a roof over my head and money to spend in my free time, if I ever had any. I told myself that it was only temporary and soon I would be able to find work as a secretary again or find a way to get to Montevideo and marry Hans Heinrich, whom I missed terribly.

Occasionally, I met with some of my friends and acquaintances from Hamburg. We were all concerned about the families we'd left behind. The situation was deteriorating in Germany. Telephone calls were almost impossible because of the time difference and because of how expensive they were; we all feared communication would be lost completely if war started. As 1939 approached, all of us hoped our loved ones could escape before it was too late.

I was happy because I had a New Year's Eve date. My employers gave me the night off, and Heinz Salfeld, whom I had known in Hamburg and dated a few times in New York, had asked me to spend New Year's Eve with him. I had no special feelings for Heinz, but I was thrilled to have the opportunity to be in New York City on New Year's Eve with somebody I knew from home.

I took the "tubes" from Newark to 34th Street in Manhattan where we'd arranged to meet. All excited, I got dolled up and headed toward the City for what I hoped would be a fun evening. Too bad neither one of us knew New York well enough to realize that there were a number of exits from the tubes on 34th Street. When I got there, I could not find Heinz. I waited for a while and then asked people whether I was really at the 34th Street exit. That's when I learned there was more than one exit. I started walking toward the other exits and, as I later learned, Heinz started doing the same thing. In that New Year's Eve crowd, we had little chance of finding each other. I was sad and disappointed not to be able to find my date, and I wondered if he had changed his mind and stood me up?

I finally gave up looking for him, and trying to make the best of it, I walked to Times Square. What an incredible scene: garish lights, masses of happy people celebrating, music blaring from stores and dance halls. It is too bad I cannot share this excitement with Heinz, I thought, but practical gal that I was I knew I did not want to spend the night alone in Times Square. I certainly did not want to go back to New Jersey to my dismal room. I decided to go to Brooklyn and surprise my friends Miggi and Fritz Ryersbach.

I had spoken to them the day before and I knew they'd be home this New Year's Eve; they'd told me I had a standing invitation to stay with them whenever I wanted to. I thought there would be just enough time to get from Times Square to their apartment before midnight. Not being a seasoned New Yorker, I didn't really know how long it would take to get to Brooklyn. And I also didn't realize that the trains didn't run as frequently on holidays as they did during the week. Unfortunately, I was all by myself in a deserted subway car when the clock struck midnight and the New Year was rung in. It was not the way I imagined I would begin the new year

I reached the Ryersbachs' at around 12:30 in the morning, and they greeted me with such holiday enthusiasm that I very quickly forgot both my missed date and my misadventures. We toasted in the New Year once more. They made me stay the night and I was very, very glad not to have to make the long trip back to New Jersey in the middle of the night. Heinz Salfeld called me after I got back home. He had apparently not fared as well as I had, and he went on and on about how upset he was about his spoiled New Year's Eve. What did he expect me to say? I never heard from him again.

My next job was with another young Jewish couple in the same neighborhood. Theirs was a much smaller apartment. I had to sleep on a convertible couch in the living room, but the apartment was light and cheerful, very much in contrast to the previous one, which was dark and gloomy. They treated me very nicely, and I found myself with a lot more free time. I did all the cleaning, washing, ironing, and cooking, but my new bosses liked simple food and never had any guests the entire time I worked there.

I enrolled in an advanced English course for foreigners at a local high school, where I went a few evenings a week. The lessons were interesting and included American history, English literature, and current events.

I had a few dates with local Jewish boys. They were all very nice to me, but I never felt very much at home with them. They seemed so naive and unsophisticated in comparison to my friends in Hamburg. I was still a foreigner, and I didn't get their jokes, didn't understand the slang, didn't know very much about American movie stars, and knew absolutely nothing about American sports like baseball, football, or basketball. Soccer and hockey, the popular European sports, weren't popular in the United States back then.

On the other hand, I absolutely loved going as a group to drive-in movies, something we did not have in Europe. How wonderful it was to sit in a car with all the windows rolled down on a balmy summer evening and watch one of the super American movies on a huge outdoor screen! I also adored going to the ice cream parlors and eating all the wonderful ice cream concoctions, which I had never seen before: sundaes with lots of whipped cream, nuts, and hot fudge; banana splits; thick malted milkshakes; and ice cream sodas. I liked the ice cream a little too much, and from a slim 110 pounds, I plumped up to 135 pounds. I looked like a blimp and none of my clothes fit anymore, so I went to a doctor who found me to be in good health but overweight. He put me on a diet. "Cut down on everything you eat," he told me, "but particularly on bread, cakes, cookies, candies, and ice cream." I followed his advice and within a few weeks I was back to my normal weight and much happier.

Chapter XX
New York, New York

Now the normally quiet Meyer household was a flurry of excitement. I had already started my second live-in housemaid job when we received word that my cousin and his wife were coming to visit.

Herta and Julius Böninger had just arrived in America. Julius hadn't seen his Aunt Berta since she left Cologne many years before. Julius was one of my mother's favorite cousins, but since he had lived in Cologne and not in Hamburg, I had never met him. I was in for a treat.

As the newest immigrant in the family, I wanted to be there to meet and greet them. After what I'd experienced, I knew first hand how important family ties are when you came to a new country. I took an immediate liking to both Herta and Julius.

Julius reminded me so much of my grandfather, my *Grosspapa*. He looked a lot like him and had his round face and sparkling eyes with the same sort of humorous twinkle *Grosspapa* had. He was chubby and spoke German with that wonderful Cologne intonation I loved so much.

Herta, in her late twenties, was an attractive young woman, with a short bob of mahogany brown hair. Quite slim, she carried herself beautifully, dressed with real flair, and on that day had on the most adorable little hat.

Hats were the fashion back then, and the cute one she wore

was a coppery color. It sat tipped forward on her head and had feather trim and a delicate little veil. Herta was very feminine and I found her easy to talk to and to get to know. She had an appealing warmth and kindness, and since she was not much older than I was we formed an immediate bond.

"We found a nicely furnished efficiency on the Westside of Manhattan," she said.

That part of the city was filled with large brownstone houses, once the homes of wealthy families, converted into small furnished rooms and apartments.

"We only have one room with a kitchenette and bath," she added. "But, Margo, whenever you want to come into New York, you can come and stay with us."

As soon as I could manage, I got a week off from my live-in maid's job and bolted over to visit.

Herta and Julius were wonderful to me. They slept on a convertible couch that opened up to a double bed, and I slept on a day bed along the other wall of the room. Herta was a great cook and like a magician, delicious meals took shape and materialized from the miniscule kitchenette. We talked continuously and got to know one another better. They knew I was not happy in Newark, and they told me to quit my job and come to New York. I couldn't believe it. Were they kidding?

"You can stay with us until you find a job here," they told me. "We can manage being cramped up for a while." They didn't have to ask twice. I could not believe my good luck; this was the break I had been waiting for. I went back to Newark and a few weeks later moved in with Julius and Herta.

Now I needed to find an office job that paid well enough for me to get out on my own. With my somewhat tenuous experience at J.J. Jacobi under my belt, I might have been a bit overconfident that my spelling and typing were good enough to land me a good secretarial job in Manhattan. I asked around and was told I needed to go to an agency and that the Kahn Agency on 42nd Street was one of the best. Dressed properly in a trim business suit, proper street pumps, hat, and gloves, I set off for the agency.

When I walked into their offices, the receptionist ordered me to wait with the other applicants in the waiting room. I was unpleasantly surprised. There must have been 200 to 300 women sitting there, waiting. Some chatted happily, some looked terrified, and others looked broken and downtrodden. They sat on uncomfortable folding chairs, row upon row. I realized what I was up against.

I said to myself, "Margo, you must be crazy, thinking you can find a job here. Here are all these New Yorkers who speak English without an accent, who went to school or even college here, and probably have many years of experience. And you want to compete with them?"

It was, after all, 1939, still the end of the Depression and jobs were hard to find even at minimal salaries.

"Oh well," I said and took a seat at the end of a long row. "I'm here. I might as well stick it out." I *was* there. I'd made the trip, I was properly dressed, I wasn't about to quit, and I knew I'd never get anywhere if I didn't try.

I persevered. I waited five hours, shifting again and again on that unforgiving chair until my turn came for an interview. The man took down all my information, told me that there were no openings at the present time, and said he would let me know if anything came up. I never heard from them again.

My next idea was to find a job where I could use my sewing skills. This time, I looked in *The New York Times* under "Help Wanted" and found an advertisement for an employment agency that was looking for seamstresses. This agency was located in a dingy walk-up on Sixth Avenue. The elevated train ran through Sixth Avenue then, and the buildings on either side of the street were old and dilapidated. It was a far cry from the gleaming sky-scraper office buildings that are there today.

A line of people waited outside the building. When I came closer, I saw that the line continued all the way up two rickety staircases to the agency's office. I went to the end. There was a big blackboard at the entrance of the building offering various jobs for men and women. Everyone was dying to land one of the few available jobs... and I got lucky.

They needed a seamstress in the alteration department of Alexander's Department Store, near the Grand Concourse in the Bronx. I didn't care what they paid me, I was overjoyed to have found a job. The next morning, I was on the subway to the 190th Street Station. I found Alexander's, and was put to work right away.

My job was to sew the hems on dresses and skirts that needed shortening. First, the fitter went in the fitting room with the customer where she pinned up and marked the hem. Another person cut off the excess, and attached a new strip of hem binding. Then it was my turn to stitch the hem by hand.

Imagine that was routine then, even for a store of low- and medium-priced garments. Today, except for Haute Couture, hemming is done by blind stitching machines, and only very high class stores feature any alteration services at all.

I had learned from my mother how to make small, precise stitches, never letting them show on the outside of the garment. That took a lot of time and certainly much longer than Alexander's alteration department allotted for stitching a hem. I was too good. At the end of the day, I was fired.

What was I going to do now? I felt uncomfortable staying on with Herta and Julius much longer, and I figured my only solution was to go back to a household job. It provided room and board and even if the salary was small--$25.00 or $30.00 per month--it was enough for the little extras I needed.

Again, I looked at the ads in *The New York Times*, and I found a job rather quickly with a family who lived in a two-bedroom apartment on Central Park West. Vladimir Vinaver had fled Russia during the Revolution and had settled in Berlin. He had met his wife, Mascha Kaléko, and they had come to New York a few years earlier. They had a little boy, Steven, who was almost two. I was hired as a combination housekeeper and nursemaid, and I slept in the room with little Steven.

Vladimir Vinaver was a choir conductor, and he must have been a very good one as he had quite a number of assignments, including concerts at Carnegie Hall.

His wife, Mascha, probably 15 or 20 years younger than Vladimir, was a lovely, vivacious, slightly mysterious and romantic woman, around 30. She had been a published writer in Berlin. Her short stories and poems described the typical Berlin characters and the city atmosphere in beautifully written German. She was trying to master English well enough, so that she could write stories about New York in English. I don't know whether she succeeded. I never came across a published work of hers in English.

Vladimir adored and spoiled her. She liked to sleep late and read a lot. Sometimes, she did a few little things around the house. Vladimir never complained and even took over most of the cooking.

I was responsible for all the housecleaning and taking care of little Steven was almost wholly my responsibility. He was a cute child, and I could

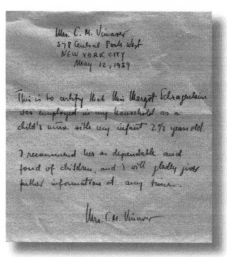

Letter of Recommendation from Mrs. Vinaver, May 12, 1939

handle him just fine when I was alone with him at home or when I took him over to Central Park, but around his parents Steven was a holy terror. He screamed, threw tantrums, and wet his pants, which, of course, I had to change.

Herta and Julius, who I still saw frequently, were sympathetic and thought they might have a solution. Some friends of Julius's from Cologne had opened up a glove factory in Manhattan. Knowing that I could operate a sewing machine, Julius thought that his friend might give me a job, and the man said, yes, he'd give me a try, but I had to see their foreman for an interview.

Mr. Berman was a handsome, charming young man, but very reluctant to hire me. I had no experience on a production line, and he could sense easily that I'd be too slow. Lothar Kaufman, Julius' friend who was one of the owners, insisted he let me try.

Experienced machine operators did very well in this arrangement called piecework. They were so fast that it seemed as if their hands and the fabric they were sewing just flew through the machine. Of course, the foreman had been correct. I was way too slow, and since you were paid according to the number of pieces you produced, I wouldn't have made enough money to live on.

Good-hearted Lothar Kaufman, took pity on me and offered me the minimum wage--25 cents per hour and a guaranteed 44-hour work week--which would bring my salary to $11.00 per week. For that, I would work part-time in the office and part-time on the sewing machine, and they would be satisfied with whatever I turned out. They hoped that with a little more experience I would get faster and more efficient, and I did.

Mr. Kaufman was very happy to have me in the office, mainly because I could write German letters for him. I was simply elated to sit behind a typewriter again, to answer a telephone, and to do some filing; I viewed it as a move up, a positive first step toward a full-time secretarial position.

But earning only $11.00 a week was okay if you lived at home, or shared a place, but living alone on that amount of money took some careful budgeting. I found a room in a big, six-story rooming house off West 85th Street between Riverside Drive and West End Avenue.

My tiny room cost $3.50 a week. It had one small window which you couldn't see out of, high up on the wall over the bed. The bed/sitter was a thin mattress on a metal frame with a throw and some pillows on it. It was a couch in the daytime, a bed at night. There was a small chest of drawers, a little table with a chair, a reading lamp and a ceiling light. I did have a sink with hot and cold water.

I shared a bathroom with others on the floor; each floor had a community kitchen. There was a telephone in each room and a switchboard downstairs. We had maid service and they changed your linens once a week, and someone at the desk downstairs made sure no uninvited visitors got into the building. Overall, the place was kept clean and pleasant. Salaries and wages were still very low, and jobs were hard to find. Some married couples even lived in rooms there. Times were tough and many people had to live like this to survive.

A bus or subway ride cost five cents. I would buy some bread, cheese, and eggs for breakfast, which I kept in the community refrigerator. For lunch, I ate a sandwich for either 10 or 15 cents and had a cup of coffee for five cents at a coffee shop near the factory. If you ate at a counter, you didn't have to tip. If I was extra hungry, I would add a small Danish to my lunch for another five cents. For dinner, one could get a plate of spaghetti or Chinese food for 25 cents. Cooking hot dogs at home and making potato salad cost about the same, 25 cents.

Even with all that penny-pinching, it was hard to live on $11.00 a week, and toward the end of the week I ate cheap cheese sandwiches for dinner or went hungry.

Chapter XXI
Doing Our Best

During this somewhat trying period, something wonderful happened to cheer me up. My dear friend from Hamburg, one of the "four-leaf-clover girls," Uschi Brager, arrived in New York with her sister and brother-in-law, Ilse and Fritz List.

Of course, they all needed to work, and Uschi found a job as a sleep-in maid with a family on Riverside Drive, just around the corner from where I lived. On her first day off, she visited and was appalled to see me living in such a dark, puny little room. But that was soon forgotten when we started talking like the good friends we were; it's impossible to describe the joy and comfort I felt having my good friend close again.

One day we were gabbing away in my room, when all of a sudden Uschi started screaming hysterically and jumped on top of the couch. I looked up and saw one of those huge flying insects from the parks along the Hudson River buzzing around the room. Uschi, terrified of bugs, was still screaming when the landlord of the building ran into the room, he thought someone was being attacked. He got a chuckle out of our damsel-in-distress commotion, and did his best to chase the bug out of my window before Uschi died of fright.

Uschi's employers liked me. When the lady gave dinner parties, I came over to help. I loved it, and the woman ended up with additional help without paying for it.

Sometimes these people went away for the weekend and I was allowed to stay with Uschi. She was a little scared to stay by herself in that big apartment; they were pleased that I could stay over, and it got me out of my own grim surroundings.

We were the most proper of house sitters. We never threw impromptu parties or ate anything we weren't supposed to eat, never drank liquor or snooped around, all common transgressions of less trustworthy live-in help.

Some nights we went to a movie together, or on a double date, and then came home to that big apartment and talked and laughed late into the night.

One fun evening, we got ravenous at about two in the morning. We went in the kitchen and we broiled four lamb chops, meant for our dinner the next evening. We hooted and laughed and devoured them, and I must say no expensive rack of lamb has ever tasted as good as those chops eaten at 2:00 a.m. with my giggly friend in that kitchen on Riverside Drive.

The Gutman-Meyer glove factory, where I was working when Uschi came, was doing well. They moved to a larger space in Brooklyn Heights. Not the pretty part of Brooklyn Heights, where the beautiful mansions look out on the ocean, but an industrialized neighborhood not too far from one of the bridges to the City.

Now it was quite an ordeal to get to work; it took much longer, and I had to walk a number of blocks from the subway station, but I had no choice. Jobs were hard to find; at least, I was lucky enough to have one.

Just a few weeks after this move, Mr. Gutman brought in a new worker who he placed at the sewing machine just opposite me. When we got a look at each other, we jumped up and fell into each other's arms with screams and laughter and tears.

Such a wild coincidence in this big city! I knew this new worker as Margot Heyman, now Margot Jarus, the older sister of one of my very good friends from Hamburg. That first night, she asked me to come home with her. She had married a doctor, from East Prussia, who had a flourishing practice before Hitler forced him to immigrate. They had come to New York a short while before, and they lived in a small apartment in the Inwood section of Manhattan.

Willy Jarus was studying to get his license to practice medicine here, and his wife, Margot, was happy to have found a job in the glove factory. For the time being, she was supporting them.

At least once or twice a week, she would ask me to come home with her to share their wonderful meals. Willy cooked. He was not only a great cook, he was an interesting and charming man. Late into the evening the three of us would have lively chats.

Finally Willy passed his medical and language tests (the latter gave him more trouble than the medical test), and they moved away to Canastota, a small town in upstate New York. Funny what you recall… the little town was famous for its onion farms. I remember when I went to see them a couple of times, always smelling the onions many miles before the train reached their station.

Willy opened his practice in this rural part of New York State as an old-fashioned country doctor. A devoted and dedicated man, he made house calls at all times of day and night, way out in the countryside in all kinds of weather. He did not mind the challenges, he thrived on them.

When World War II broke out, he volunteered for the army; he worked in an army hospital in Dayton, Ohio. We were great friends by that time, and I vis-

Willy and Margot Jarus with
their daughter, Linda

ited them there and again when they moved to Syracuse, NY, where they bought themselves a big house, adopted a baby girl, and Willy opened his practice on the ground floor of their new home.

Willy died many, many years ago at age 62. His dear wife, Margot, never remarried. She stayed quite active and died shortly after her 91st birthday, in June 2003, ending our relationship of more than seventy years.

When I think back about many of the people I knew who fled Hitler, I believe America made out very well. Europe's loss was our gain; so many good and talented people came here during the same period I did. They stayed to make a difference here, to give their hearts and souls and their intelligence to the country that gave them their freedom.

Chapter XXII
Fred

Although I was still a little in love with Hans Heinrich, our chances of ever being together were slim. I thought it was time to move on and meet someone new. Anyway, I was lonely. One of the girls at the glove factory wanted to arrange a date for me with a fellow refugee from Germany, and I agreed.

Fred was tall, slightly over six feet, not really handsome, but attractive nonetheless. I liked the fact that he was extremely well dressed in tailor-made suits with matching shirts and ties. His slightly thinning brown hair was parted on the left and was well-cut and neatly combed. His small, brown eyes danced and sparkled. To tell you the truth, I haven't the faintest idea where we went on our first date, but I recall that he had sophisticated manners, talked intelligently, and had an endearing, sheepish

Fred

smile. He was 37 years old, 17 years older than I, but that really didn't bother me.

Fred liked me, too, because he called me the next day and asked for another date. He lived in a furnished room on 135th Street and Riverside Drive. I had moved in with my friend Lilo Hirt and her mother and sister on 137th Street near Amsterdam Avenue, so we lived conveniently close to each other.

Fred told me he'd earned a good income in Berlin as a sales manager for a manufacturer of fine men's shirts in the northern part of Germany. As a sideline, he and his girlfriend, Terry, who was a model, created and managed fashion shows for high priced ladies wear. After Terry left him for unexplained reasons, he met and married a very attractive blonde woman by the name of Marietta. I remember her name because Fred gave me quite a few of her handkerchiefs, which were embroidered with the letter "M."

Fred

Fred told me tearfully that his dear Marietta had fled Hitler's Germany to England and was killed in London during the Blitz. Fred, himself, had immigrated easily to New York because he was an American citizen. His German-born father had immigrated to America as a young man and had become an American citizen, but he'd wanted to marry a girl from his own background so he went back to Berlin where he met and married Fred's mother.

She was from an affluent Jewish family, who didn't want their daughter to go to America, and they offered Fred's father a position in their business; the young couple stayed in Berlin. Since Fred was born in Berlin of a father who was a United States citizen, Fred had the option when he reached the age of 21 of either remaining a German citizen or becoming an American. He opted for the American citizenship and therefore had no difficulties coming to America. We never discussed why Marietta had fled to England instead of coming with him.

We dated for about two years. In a way, I felt sorry for Fred. His English was very poor, and all he could find were low paying messenger jobs; he was too smart for that. We tried to figure out a way to help him advance.

Margo and Fred on a bench in Central Park, NYC, 1939

He was good to me, eager to be kind, and he took me to nice places. I found out later he was in debt, borrowing money he very often never paid back. But ignorance is bliss, and in the meantime we had fun. Fred was a great dancer and there were many places owned by former Germans or Austrians where you could dance every night and Sunday afternoons, too, to European bands that played our beloved, well-known melodies.

Fred was ambitious and much too intelligent to be a mere messenger boy. He asked me one day, "Don't you think we could produce fashion shows, the way I used to in Berlin?"

We knew quite a few German and Austrian immigrants who had dress shops and handbag stores, who also sold jewelry and other accessories, and we knew quite a few milliners. In those days, hats were very much in style. Even I, with my meager salary, had hats made to order and spent more for them than I did for my ready-made dresses. Furthermore, we knew all the European coffee houses and dance clubs where we could hold our fashion shows either for free or for just a small payment. Usually, these establishments would advertise the fashion shows to attract more customers who, of course, also ate and drank during the show. They loved the additional business that these shows created for them.

Margo and Fred

Fred advertised for the models and we found some cute ones who were happy to work for us in their spare time. Both of us went around on evenings and weekends to the various stores to get the proper items for our productions. It was a lot of work, but it was also a lot of fun. We charged a small admission fee, and we also received a percentage on everything that was sold at the show. Fred was the announcer and I helped dress the models. But after only two or three shows, we saw that in addition to not making any money, we could barely cover our expenses. We even had trouble paying the models. It was an embarrassing situation when the poor models called me at my job trying to collect their money. We reluctantly admitted that fashion shows were not a profitable business, at least for us, and we started looking for something else.

Fred tried selling European delicacies. He bought the supplies and sold them. One evening, we were quietly sitting on his couch, when. BANG! Pop! Pow! some of the *Himbeersaft* bottles blew up and made an awful foamy mess. That was the end of that. He then got himself a job in a delicatessen and later on worked in a chocolate shop.

After a while, I became completely disenchanted with Fred, especially when I found out what a liar he was. I had never experienced such dishonesty. I could not believe it when I learned that his long-lamented Marietta was no more dead than I was. She was walking around in England, sans a few embroidered handkerchiefs, which she probably missed more than she missed Fred.

Imagine his lying about her and playing on my sympathy all that time. What possessed him? I just didn't like being used that way. I also found that he owed many people a lot of money, that he was not making a living, and that he habitually skipped out on his rent, moving from one furnished room to another without paying.

He began to scare me. Finding him so untrustworthy changed my way of thinking and I wanted to be rid of him. I couldn't imagine how I'd been so taken in. It shook me up a little, and I vowed to be on my guard and maybe, just maybe, think about taking my mother's advice once in a while. She instinctively had pegged Fred as a bad prospect.

One evening when I met Fred for drinks at a bar, I finally told him that I did not want to see him anymore. He pleaded with me to change my mind. "As soon as I can get Marietta to give me a divorce, I will marry you," he pleaded. By then, I wanted no part of his lies.

But Fred, in spite of his shortcomings, could definitely attract women. Trude, his second wife, was older than I had been when she met Fred. She married him and they had a son, but I guess he disappointed her, too, as she divorced him only three years later. She ended up marrying my future husband Henry's best friend, Paul.

Trude and I became close friends. We shared and appreciated the fact that we had both been in love with Fred. She told me Fred's version of his last date with me, and I listened both amazed and amused. "I had this girlfriend, Margo," he had told Trude, "and I wanted to break up with her. We met for drinks, and when I told her it was over between us, she pulled a small gun with a mother-of-pearl handle out of her pocketbook and she tried to shoot me! Fortunately, I grabbed the gun away from her, the crazy fool, and later on I threw the darn thing in the Hudson River."

Trude and I laughed hysterically over this typical fabrication by Fred. One thing that wasn't very funny--and that he couldn't lie about--was that he got very sick with terrible diabetes and died a young man.

Chapter XXIII
Working Girl

While working daytime in the glove factory, I started attending night school. I thought it would be a good idea to brush up on my office skills and I wanted to get a better grasp of accounting and bookkeeping. With my abilities at a new level, I wanted to land a decent secretarial job. Through a relative of Margot and Willy Jarus, I finally landed my first office job in New York.

Herbert Feist interviewed me at his business in an old building at 84 University Place, in the Village. When University Place had been a fashionable "uptown" address for well-to-do New Yorkers, this had been a luxury apartment building. Now, however, a few manufacturers, small businesses, shops, antique stores, and book dealers occupied the busy street. There were also a number of small restaurants just a few blocks away, frequented by the students of New York University. It was a lively atmosphere in spite of the older, run-down buildings.

Herbert Feist was in his early forties, a handsome, soft-spoken man with a head of prematurely gray hair. He was kind and pleasant, and he told me that he had recently emigrated from Germany with his wife and two small children. He had been a banker in Germany, working in his father's bank, planning one day to take over the business. Of course, after Hitler came to power, the business was confiscated and the family had to leave their native Manheim to escape the fate of many Jews who were killed in concentration camps.

Even more impressive, Herbert Feist was also an artist. He could paint and sculpt. Somehow, through his contact with the art world, he had obtained a license to manufacture a special kind of paint, which would give picture frames and sculptures an antique appearance.

This special paint and other necessary ingredients like gold leaf, lacquers, and brushes were assembled into kits and sold to art supply stores. We produced the paint in a small factory adjoining the offices where I was interviewed; the kits were also assembled and shipped from there.

After giving me a short typing test, Mr. Feist hired me to handle all the office work. I answered the phones, wrote letters, billed customers, and oversaw the bookkeeping. He hired me with the following warning: "While you have no American office experience, I will give you the chance to work here. But you must promise me not to leave after six months when you feel you have improved your skills." I promised and I stayed with him until the firm went out of business two years later. My starting salary was $12.00 per week.

In the end, it turned out to be an interesting job. Herbert Feist had a partner, who I assumed had financed the business. He, too, was a German-Jewish immigrant who had managed to escape from Germany with some money. He was rather stiff and formal in contrast to Herbert Feist's easy-going manner, and the two of them had their disagreements, often about business and about politics. While

Franklin Delano Roosevelt

Feist was a Democrat, his partner was a Republican.

Franklin Delano Roosevelt was running for president against Wendell Willkie that year, and when the Sunday magazine section of *The New York Times* displayed FDR's picture on its front page one week, Herbert Feist pasted the picture on cardboard and hung it in the entrance hall of our office. When Wendell Willkie's picture graced the cover of *The New York Times* magazine the next week, Feist's partner pasted it on the back of the cardboard and turned the sign. My two bosses, usually grown-up businessmen, started acting like little children. And from then on, it was the same routine:

Wendell Willkie

every morning, whoever came in first would turn the picture to the side of his candidate, and as soon as the other partner arrived he would reverse it. This continued until Election Day 1940, when FDR was re-elected to his third term in office.

The two men also argued, violently sometimes, about how the business should be run. I was much too young and inexperienced at the time to know who was right, but I remember that one of the arguments got so heated that my boss's partner threw a bottle of expensive liquid gold leaf at him. Fortunately for Feist, he ducked.

Actually, the job had some very enjoyable aspects. I made a good friend of the young chemist who ran the factory and he became my friend and confidante. He was happily married and we were just good friends. On the other hand, Feist tried very hard to develop a romantic relationship with me. Luckily, with a little humor, I was able to discourage his efforts without losing my job.

What I liked best was attending the trade shows a few times a year. I demonstrated how our little kits were used to make beautiful antique-looking and modern frames. I must admit I really don't have any artistic talents at all, but I became quite good at finishing sample frames and sculptures. It was also great fun to meet the fascinating, "artsy" people at these shows.

Since the partners were quite satisfied with my work, they raised my salary a few times while I worked there, always at the rate of 50 cents per week, which even in 1940 was not enough to help very much. Somehow, I scraped along. I do not remember whether the business eventually failed or whether the partners couldn't manage to get along anymore or what happened, but they liquidated the business approximately two years after I started working there.

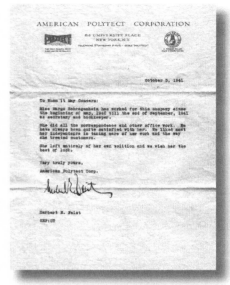

Recommendation letter from Herbert Feist

Herbert Feist opened up a shop finishing and restoring pictures and frames for galleries and museums. After a while, he also opened a gallery on Madison Avenue selling paintings and other artwork, but he always kept up with the restoration work. He stayed in touch with me and occasionally asked me to moonlight, handling some bookkeeping for him. I never fell prey to his amorous advances, and we stayed good friends until he died a number of years ago.

Chapter XXIV
The Kunstlers

Forty-Seventh Street is the center of the diamond trade in New York City. Every store window glitters with jewelry and loose stones. It was much the same in the 1940s; diamond dealers occupied almost every building, and the smaller stores were either on 47th Street, between Fifth and Sixth Avenues, or just around the corner on Fifth Avenue and 47th Street. It was a tantalizing, mysterious microcosm and there I sat, right smack dab in the middle of it.

I had finally secured the enviable position of full-fledged book-keeper. And not just at any Mom and Pop business. I was working for William Kunstler, a preeminent diamond dealer at 62 West 47th Street. In fact, Kunstler had been called the "Diamond King" before the Depression. Imagine that, I was now working for the "Diamond King!"

According to gossip on "the Street," as 47th Street was called, Kunstler had lost most of his money in the 1929 Crash, but some-how he'd managed to survive and was happily wheeling and deal-ing again when I started working for him. He was a short, stocky man, in his early sixties, and he spoke English with a heavy Jew-ish-Polish accent. He was jovial and good-natured, and we took an immediate liking to each other. His four sons were also in the business. Today, the diamond trade is still centered on 47th Street, but the gem trading business has very much changed. Back then, trading literally took place on the streets of the Diamond District, not just in the offices and in the stores.

The area took shape in the 1920's, and the diamond business was dominated primarily by Yiddish- speaking Orthodox or Hasidic Jews who wore long black frock coats and wide-brimmed black hats. Some had long beards, some just the long ringlet side locks or "peyos" hair, growing from their temples. Among other arcane things about them was the way they did business. On the Street, inside or out, their word was their bond.

A man would take a small, folded paper, a *briefke*, which contained loose diamonds held securely within its folds, from inside his deep pockets. Adroitly, he would open it and show the stones to his prospective customer. No one ever dropped the diamonds out of the creased paper parcel, no matter how tiny they were. I always wondered how they kept them from blowing away in the cross-town winds, no doubt some protective cupping of the hands learned at their father's knee.

The diamond seller and his customer would bargain about the price and if they agreed on the worth of the stones, the seller would refold the *briefke*, handing it immediately over to the buyer. They would shake hands and say, *"Mazel Und Broche"* (Good Luck and Blessings). This meant the deal was sealed, and the buyer would pay the arranged price. Nobody ever went back on such a deal. Nowadays, however, you see fewer deals made on the streets. It still happens, but not as before. Security is tighter now. More paperwork is required. A lot of the mystery, intrigue, and charm are gone, but the diamond merchants still live by their code.

William Kuntsler's oldest son, Charlie, was the most charming of his children. He was divorced and had an adorable seven year-old son of his own who lived with the child's mother, a young, pretty blonde. Charlie lived in the fashionable East Sixties between Fifth and Madison Avenues in one of those beautiful patrician homes that had been converted into apartment complexes. Charlie was tall with reddish-blondish hair, very charming, definitely a man about town. A string of attractive women came in and out of his life, and some of them made an occasional appearance at the office. Charlie liked me and flirted with me a little. He talked to me about his personal life, and he even sent me postcards from his various trips. I had the feeling he was tempted to ask me for a date with the prospect of starting an affair with me, but the fact that I worked in the office and was considerably younger than he was must have held him back.

Albert was the next oldest son. He was single and only made occasional appearances at the office. He sold diamonds for the company in various parts of the country. Mike, the third son, worked in the office, too; he was quiet but pleasant. He was married to a woman whose father owned a diamond mine in South America, and he lived a pampered, comfortable life.

Henry, the youngest son, was the most solid of the bunch. He was married, had two small children, and lived in suburban New Jersey. He suffered from a back ailment, which probably accounted for his somewhat grouchy disposition, but he treated me well and trusted me completely. And trust was very important in the diamond business.

The Kunstlers carried a sizeable amount of inventory in diamonds of all sizes, shapes, and qualities. After I had been there just a little while, they let me close the office in the afternoon after everyone had left. This entailed closing the safe, which held all the diamonds, and activating the alarm system. I was well aware what trust in me this duty implied.

Quite a few times, I worried and asked myself, "Did I close the safe properly? Did I activate the alarm?" Obsessively, I would come back after I had already walked to the subway, checking just to make sure.

To my satisfaction and peace of mind, I always did the job properly and everything remained safe. I was also entrusted with packages of diamonds to deliver from our office to prospective buyers. It never occurred to me that I might be held up and robbed, but this was in the 1940's when life in New York was a whole lot safer than it is today.

The job was fascinating. I not only handled their bookkeeping, but sometimes they let me help sort the diamonds. They showed me how to use a jeweler's loop, how to weigh diamonds, and I learned the various cuts, colors, imperfections, and other details of the diamond trade. Their specialty was buying estate jewelry: bracelets, necklaces, and sometimes tiaras. They called these "breakers" because they would destroy the beautiful jewelry with pliers just to keep the diamonds. The diamonds would then be sorted

Margo sorting diamonds, 47th Street, NYC, 1941

according to size, shape, color, and quality and added to our inventory, while the scrap gold and platinum were sold to smelters.

The Kunstlers sold their diamonds to a number of other wholesale dealers who needed particular qualities and/or sizes, but they also sold to jewelry manufacturers and to retail jewelry stores all over the country. Retail meant good profits, but the retail stores were notoriously slow payers. Most clients paid by drafts extending over a period of three to six months--sometimes even longer--and they often asked for payment extensions. On top of that, sometimes our sales people had to visit customers personally to collect. However, I cannot recall more than one or two bankruptcies during the three years I worked there.

The people who came to our office--mostly other diamond dealers--were fascinating characters from all over Europe. Most of them were very nice to me and helped me speak and understand some "Jiddish." It was strange to them that even though I was a Jew I did not know this language. But Yiddish was a language used mostly by Jews in the Eastern European countries and hardly ever by German Jews like me.

One of the men who came to our office quite regularly was a moneylender by the name of Joe Noah. He could neither read nor write, and I have no idea how he obtained the money he was lending. I also don't know why these diamond dealers couldn't go to banks for loans. I think they often did, but could not get all the money they needed. Joe Noah came in handy. He would lend out a certain amount against a note and let me figure the interest on the transaction. Then he would go to a bookkeeper at another firm and make sure my figures were correct. Conversely, I checked the figures of other bookkeepers. He was a kind man and at the end of the year he would always show his appreciation with a nice monetary gift. I understand that Joe Noah died in his nineties as a multimillionaire without ever learning to read or write.

But the most interesting character of all of them was William Kunstler himself. He was born in Galicia, which was then part of the Austro-Hungarian Empire and is now Poland. Despite being Jewish he went to a German school, and when I met him he could still read and write German as well as recite parts of the German classic poems from *Goethe* and *Schiller*. When he was 17, he was drafted into the army, but instead he fled the country and settled in Antwerp, Belgium, the center of the international diamond trade. At the age of 18, he met and married the daughter of a local diamond dealer. His father-in-law took him into his business and since he was a bright, young man he learned quickly. During World War I, he left Belgium, lived in South Africa for a while, then in Paris, and finally settled in New York. He also fathered six children, the four boys and two girls. Helen, who was the first-born, was divorced by the time I came into the business. Lenore was the youngest, and she was newly married when I met her. She insisted on telling me graphic stories about her sex life. Why, I'll never know?

Unfortunately, William Kunstler's wife had died giving birth to her last child and he was a young widower with six children. However, since money was no problem, he had housekeepers and nannies to help raise the children.

The stock market crash of 1929 had practically bankrupted him, but he was determined to bounce back again and he did. By the time I started working for him, he had been remarried for quite a number of years to a former bookkeeper by the name of Bea who his boys detested. She came from a poor home on the lower East side of Manhattan and the boys were afraid she married their father for his money. Helen, William Kunstler's oldest child, who was older than Bea, hated her. To make things worse, there were two more children from this second marriage, a boy and a girl. They were eight and ten years old and spoiled. They lived in a beautiful home in Deal, New Jersey, which was one of the more affluent towns on the New Jersey coast.

William Kunstler seemed very content, even while his older children remained very angry. I was invited to spend the weekend with them in Deal several times. Bea was a pleasant woman, a good hostess, and nice to her husband and to her children and me.

William Kunstler, however, was an eccentric character. He never carried any money on him. Since he knew so many people on the Street and was very well liked, he obviously felt he could always borrow what he needed when he needed to. Indeed, that would often happen. Sometimes, when we worked late, he would ask me to have dinner with him. He would hail a taxi-cab, and before closing the car's door he would yell to one of the fellows on the Street, "Please lend me some cash (at least enough for a good dinner for two)." He would always get what he needed, and obviously he always paid it back.

His sons laughed at his antics, but they all made sure to get equal parts of the business. I always had the distinct feeling that they didn't trust one another. They also didn't like it that the old man paid a lot of attention to me. One bookkeeper in the family was enough for them (I heard), but they didn't have to be afraid. There was no romance between the two of us. I left this very interesting family and this very well paying job after three years to try living in California. I turned over the job to my friend Lilo Hirt, who also enjoyed working for the

Lilo Hirt, school friend,
NYC, 1941

Letter of Recommendation from
William Kunstler

Kuntslers. I heard many years later that after the old man died, the boys had a hard time managing the business and eventually they went bankrupt.

"Mazel Und Broche" always takes me back to those days in the Diamond District. I can't see a jewelry store window today without thinking of the "Diamond King" and my time spent on 47th Street.

"A Sheynem dank." Thank you very much, Mr. William Kunstler, a truly unforgettable character.

Chapter XXV
My Family Escapes

In May of 1939, my parents and my sister, Vera, managed to escape to London. Life under the Nazi regime had become more and more unbearable, and war was imminent. Hitler had taken control of Czechoslovakia in March of that year, and there were rumors that Poland would be his next target. England and France might very well decide to help Poland, and if that happened there would certainly be war. Daddy felt that they could not risk being caught in Germany, that Jews would be the first to suffer. Hans Enoch, Daddy's cousin, helped him get permission to enter England.

After all the arrangements were made, Daddy, Mutti, and Vera said tearful goodbyes to our family and friends who were still in Hamburg. Some of Daddy's friends could not understand why he was leaving. "This regime will collapse," they told him. "You will see. This cannot last and democracy will return."

"If that should happen and I certainly hope it does," Daddy answered them, "I can always come back. But in the meantime, I want to make sure that my family and I are safe." A week later, they sailed on the *S.S. Manhattan* to England.

The German government did not permit Jews who left the country to take any money or other valuables with them. After staying with Hans Enoch and his mother in London for a few days, they had to find work. Through the Jewish Committee, they found a solution. A job was found for both Mutti and for Daddy as a sleep-in domestic couple with a British family. Mutti would be the cook and Daddy the butler and chauffeur. If it hadn't been so sad, it would have been funny. Our dear Mutti was certainly not one of the best cooks, and Daddy throughout his life had only known what it was like to be waited *on*. But they were fairly young, still in their early forties, and could take adversities in stride. Most of all, they had to save their lives and that of my sister.

For Vera, the solution was to live with a Quaker family, with a mother, a father, and a daughter who was Vera's age. The family had offered to take a refugee child and treat her as a member of their family as long as it was necessary. And they really did make Vera part of the family; they sent her to school and helped her learn English.

I was trying desperately to arrange my family's immigration to America. I went to the Council of Jewish Women, an organization that helped people with immigration applications. The Meyers were perfectly willing to provide the affidavits, but the very nice woman at the Council told me that the Immigration Service would not accept any more immigration affidavits from Charles Meyer. He had already signed twelve affidavits for relatives from his side of the family, plus the one for me, and, therefore, he could no longer sponsor anyone else.

"What am I going to do now?" I asked the lady at the Council. "War might break out in Europe any day, and then my parents will be stuck in England." The woman told me she would try to find us some help and to call her in about two weeks. It was an agonizing wait, but when I called I got wonderful news.

She had convinced her lawyer-husband to sponsor my family, provided I could assure her that they would not come to them for any kind of help after their arrival in the United States. I told this kind woman, "Nobody in our family will ever become a burden to you. Both my parents are in their early forties, healthy, and willing to work. There never will be a problem. I promise."

England and France declared war on Germany on September 1, 1939, after Hitler's troops started their assault on Poland. Now I was afraid that Mutti, Daddy, and Vera might not be able to leave England; the Atlantic might become too dangerous.

My fears increased when tragedy struck my mother's brother, Martin, his wife, Minnie, and their son, Walter. The three had received permission to immigrate to Chile. They had booked passage on the *S.S. Simon Bolivar*. Uncle Martin had been in a concentration camp for a while, but, at that time, men who could produce proof that they had permission to immigrate to another country were still being released. Aunt Minnie had obtained their papers and Uncle Martin was released from the camp.

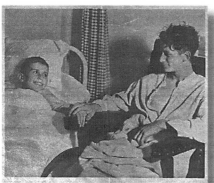

And still they smile. Walter Boenenger (left), 11, gets a hand pat from J. S. Mullen, engineer on the Bolivar. The boy, ironically, is a German. Two Nazi mines blasted the ship.

Walter Böninger and a crew member of the *Simon Bolivar* in the hospital after the sinking of the ship

Just two days after boarding, their ship hit a German mine in the English Channel and was blown up. Many passengers perished, including Uncle Martin and Aunt Minnie. British rescue boats found their son, Walter, who was eleven years old. He'd been pulled from the sea so completely covered with oil that he appeared to be black. They brought him ashore and put him into a hospital. My parents heard about the *Simon Bolivar*, and Mutti was beside herself. "That is the ship Martin, Minnie, and the boy just took," she began screaming.

The news was shattering, but they finally found Walter and the authorities brought them together. Mutti and Daddy took care of him but a fight with Walter's maternal grandparents erupted over his custody. They had fled to Belgium, where they hoped to survive the war, but it was clear that Hitler's troops would sooner or later try to occupy Belgium, Holland, and Luxembourg. My parents were afraid to let Walter go there. With the help of lawyers and sympathetic authorities, Mutti got permission to become Walter's guardian and to take him with her to the United States.

Chapter XXVI

Reunion at Grand Central Station

I n August of 1940, Mutti, Daddy, and Vera were finally able to board a ship to Halifax, Canada. It was a long and difficult trip, and in order to avoid mines, the ship took a longer route. A surveillance convoy accompanied them, the last to accompany a passenger ship until the end of the war in 1945.

While Walter could not go with them, Mutti did manage to get him on a children's transport, which followed a few days later. Daddy sent me a telegram the minute they arrived in Halifax.

I was so happy to know that the three of them would soon be on American soil. They came by train to Grand Central Station in New York, and I was waiting for them on the platform. We hugged and kissed. It was hard to believe that my family was finally reunited--safely--in my adopted home, New York City.

Chapter XXVII
Toledo, Ohio

"We have arrived in Halifax, boarding the train for New York," the telegram from my father read. "Tomorrow arriving at Grand Central Station 4:30 in the afternoon." They were safe now. I was going to see my family again. I took Fred with me to the train station so that he could help with the luggage and make sure that nothing would be lost or stolen in the general commotion of their arrival. It turned out to be a mistake. My mother took an immediate disliking to Fred. I really don't know why and I didn't learn about my mother's distaste for Fred until much later. I was so happy to see the three of them again, especially my little sister, Vera, who looked much more mature and even prettier than when I'd last seen her before I left.

I had rented them a furnished room on 140th Street and Broadway, not far from were I lived. I thought it looked quite pleasant when I rented it, and besides I could hardly afford to pay for anything more expensive on my very meager wages. The room turned out to be infested with bed bugs, and they all spent a rather uncomfortable night. I took them to a Chinese restaurant at the corner of 145th Street and Broadway, and Daddy was amazed at what a wonderful seven-course dinner we were served for sixty-five cents per person. It was 1940. Wages were low and naturally so was the cost of living.

My mother found accommodations that were a little better and started to keep house for her family, but she was not at all happy with her surroundings. In the meantime, Daddy contacted some of his friends who had been in New York for a while in the hope that they could help him find a job. Things were still rather tough. America had not quite worked itself out of the Depression and jobs were hard to find, especially for new immigrants who had limited knowledge of the English language and no experience in the American business world. Some of the new immigrants were running freight elevators in industrial buildings, some were cleaners in factories, and many worked in Klein's on the Square, the only self-service clothing store at the time. In fact, it was a completely self-service store without any sales help at all. Women who shopped there had the habit of throwing clothing they did not want on the floor or in disarray on the counters. So Klein's hired men to pick the clothes up and to put everything in the right place. But Daddy could not see himself doing such a job.

On the suggestion of a friend, he went to the Council of Jewish Women who were helping resettle new immigrants in other parts of the United States. He was told that there was a nice Jewish community in Racine, Wisconsin, which had advised the Council that they would be happy to take care of a Jewish immigrant family. Daddy, Mutti, and Vera decided to leave New York in the hope that life would be more pleasant in a smaller community. They also hoped that Daddy would find a job there. I was sorry to see them go so soon after their arrival, but now they were safely in America and I hoped that after a while I could visit with them again.

On a very hot August day, they left New York to travel by bus to their new destination. The bus was not air-conditioned and it took thirty-six hours to reach Milwaukee, Wisconsin, where they had to change to a local bus to Racine. Obviously, it was a long and arduous ride, and the three of them arrived in Milwaukee completely exhausted and in need of a bath and a bed. The bus driver had let them off at a gas station, where they were supposed to catch another bus to Racine. Daddy began talking to the owner of the gas station in order to make sure that they would be catching the right bus to Racine. Daddy told the man that he was a refugee from Nazi Germany. "Too bad!" the man answered. "Hitler should have thrown all the Jews in the ocean. It would be a better world!" he added. What a welcome to America!

On the other hand, their reception in Racine was very

German Refugee Comes to Park After 15 Months' Stay in England

"At first I thought I was in a dream," exclaimed Vera Schrag, Jewish refugee from Germany, in describing her first impression of America.

This 16-year old, brown-haired, attractive girl is Park's most recent newcomer. Commenting on her life in Germany, Vera said, "We Jews were not allowed to go to the public schools nor were we admitted to theaters, swimming pools, or libraries. Before we left the country our radio, bicycles, car, money, silverware, and jewelry were taken from us."

Tells of Experiences

Since leaving Hamburg, her home in Germany, Vera has spent 15 months in England and three weeks in New York before coming to Racine where she has been for four weeks, two of which she has spent at Park.

Telling of her experiences Vera exclaimed, "We spent two years trying to get out of Germany. Because so many wanted to leave we had to wait until our quota number was called. After some difficulty we secured passage on the liner Washington for England. While in England my parents and I lived in London and Essex, and I learned the English language."

Hopes to Make Friends

Continuing the account of her experiences, Vera said, "We came from England with a convoy. The trip took 16 days instead of the usual five or six, and the sea was very rough. We landed in Canada. From there we took a train to New York, where my sister has been working for the past

Introducing Vera Schrag, German-Jewish refugee.

comment on Racine. "It's like Hamburg, only smaller." The Schrags were sent to Racine by a committee for the placing of German Jewish refugees.

Naming sewing as one of her hobbies, Vera continued, "I don't think the Germans dress up as much as the Americans."

Closing the interview, she stated, with her charming smile, "I love to read English. I am going to read that now, not German. We have taken out our first citizenship papers, and will be citizens of this country in five years."

Vera's story

friendly. They were the first German-Jewish family that the Racine Jewish Community had sponsored, and the Jews of Racine went out of their way to make Daddy, Mutti, and Vera feel comfortable. They provided a nicely furnished apartment for them, and Vera immediately entered the local high school where she became a celebrity and a sensation. The editor of the school paper interviewed her and published the write-up accompanied by Vera's picture. Mutti let everyone know that she was a dressmaker, so they provided her with a sewing machine, and soon thereafter she started making beautiful clothes for the women of the community. These Jewish women of Racine were thrilled and were happy to march down the aisles of the synagogue during the High Holy Days showing off their newly acquired finery. But poor Daddy still could not find a job. Nobody wanted to hire him because he had no American business experience. They should have given him a chance, of course. He was a top salesman and, as he proved later, very successful in fields completely unrelated to his previous experience. In fact, he was still young, in his mid-forties, spoke English, and was very adaptable. He went to the head of the Jewish community and told him, "I appreciate greatly what you have done for my family and for me, but I cannot live on charity. I am really willing to do any type of work to earn a living." But it did not help, and Daddy finally took the steps necessary to change this situation.

On the ship traveling from England to Canada, Daddy had befriended a man who was planning to settle in Toledo, Ohio. They had exchanged names--the man's name was Mr. Nelson--and other personal information. One day, Daddy called him and told him how unhappy he was about not finding any work in Racine. "Come to Toledo," Mr. Nelson suggested, "I think I can find you a job here." Mr. Nelson had become the caretaker of the only Jewish country club in Toledo, and he had met quite a number of substantial business people. "If you come to Toledo," he said, "I am convinced that through my connections at the club you will find a job."

Within a few days after that, Daddy went by train to Toledo, and a few days later he landed a job in a steel warehouse. It was hard work for my poor dad. He had to carry steel bars from one place to another and load them on trucks. He certainly was not used to that kind of physical work, but somehow he managed. He was glad to earn a living, although it was not very much money. He found and rented a furnished apartment and not too long after his arrival in Toledo, Mutti and Vera were able to join him. Daddy did not stay very long at the steel company. He got himself a job as a salesman behind the cigarette counter at Lanes Drug Store. He was so happy to be back in an activity that he knew and loved.

Shortly thereafter, he joined a firm in the home improvement business, and he again became a very successful salesperson. Vera finished high school and became a riveter in an airplane factory. Unfortunately, it did not last very long. We were at war and she was working in an essential war industry, but she was not yet an American citizen and they discovered that they had actually made a mistake by hiring her in the first place. One day, a supervisor came and in the middle of the workday Vera was escorted out of the factory. They put her to work in another part of the factory, and, after a while, she helped sell furniture in one of the finer stores in Toledo. She did very well, except when she made the mistake of trying to sell a "sexual" couch instead of a "sectional" couch. Mutti had gone back to her dressmaking profession, and the three of them were a happy family again.

I visited from New York every holiday and during my vacations. I traveled by train since there were no airplane connections to Toledo, and, in all likelihood, I could not have afforded the airfare anyway. It was a twelve-to-fourteen-hour ride during the night, and I certainly could not afford a sleeper compartment. But it was always wonderful being together with the family. Mutti tried very hard to convince me to move to Toledo. She found job offerings and dates with men for me, and whenever I left she looked at me with sad eyes and asked, "Can't you just give it a try?" I would always answer, "No, Mutti, Toledo is not for me." By then, I was used to my freedom and to life in the big city. I found Toledo and the people I met there rather provincial and mostly dull. There was too much gossip and small talk. In spite of my loving family, I just could not see myself ever living in that kind of environment.

Chapter XXVIII
California, Here I Come

My sister's engagement was the big news in the family. Vera and Louis were getting married, as soon as the war was over and he was out of the Air Force, that is. While in the service, Louis had met some men who told him how wonderful life in California was, and he wrote Vera that he thought it would be a good idea to live there after they were married. My mother, in Toledo, was not at all happy about the idea of having one daughter living in New York on the East Coast and another one in California on the West Coast. Her solution was for me to move to Los Angeles, where my cousins, Julius and Herta Böninger, had settled.

Mother said I would have no trouble finding a job as a bookkeeper out there--what an optimist she was--and I could also look for employment possibilities for my father. I knew, of course, that her ulterior motive was to get me away from Henry, who I'd been dating for a number of years. I knew she wanted to get me back in circulation. Mother felt I was wasting my time with Henry.

By this time, I'd been dating Henry for three or four years, and although I loved him dearly I, too, was disappointed that he had not proposed. I wasn't even sure he wanted to marry me. He was in his mid-thirties, and he seemed to be a confirmed bachelor. Perhaps my parents were right, I thought, to send me far away from him? In any case, it was 1944 and my adventurous spirit took over and I said to myself, "California, Here I Come."

Always the adventurer, and sincerely liking the idea of us all being together in any city other than Toledo--which I thought provincial and dull--I followed their suggestion. I quit my job, packed all my belongings in two suitcases, and took a train to Toledo. After a week visiting my parents and Vera, I took another train to Chicago, and from there I boarded a bus headed for San Francisco.

However, this was still wartime, and air traffic was almost exclusively reserved for military personnel. The train or bus was the only way to travel long distances.

Moreover, a bus trip of that magnitude held some interest for me--I would see America--but I really had no idea how big America was and what a grueling ordeal a cross country trip would be. Naïve and inexperienced as I was, I figured that at the end of each day, I would get off the bus, sleep in a nearby hotel or motel, and then continue the next morning on another bus. It never occurred to me that it was not at all the way it worked.

On the first day, after leaving Chicago and going through Illinois and Iowa, we reached Nebraska's endless corn and wheat fields. We drove for miles and miles without even seeing a farmhouse, eventually resting at a dinky lunch stop. I feared I was due for yet another unattractive surprise at dinner.

As evening approached, I spoke to the bus driver about my idea of staying overnight. "Are you kidding?" he said. "We won't see a hotel on this route till we hit Colorado tomorrow."

At our dinner stop, my fears were confirmed. Outside of the lonely looking diner, there seemed to be nothing else around but a small village and more unending wheat fields.

The night on the bus was miserable. I felt filthy and I couldn't sleep.

When we got to Denver the next day, I'd had enough, and I decided to get off the bus, find a nice hotel, take a shower, change my clothes, and get a good night's sleep. The bus stopped not far from what seemed to be the center of the city--a large square sur-rounded by a number of hotels. I went into the nicest one and told the reception clerk, "I am Margo Shrag. I sent you a telegram requesting a room." He looked through his records, and, of course, found no telegram. There was also no room. I looked disheveled from two days and two nights on the bus, certainly not the type of guest desired at a good hotel.

I tried the same approach in three other hotels, but without success. I eventually learned that there was a large air base right outside Denver, and every Saturday all hotels were booked by the friends and families of the airmen.

Then I remembered that some distant relatives by the name of Levinsohn lived in Denver, and I found their name in the telephone book and called them. Remembering that they were very Orthodox Jews, I was afraid they might not answer the tele-phone on Shabbat, but luck was with me and Mrs. Levinsohn picked up the phone.

The Levinsohns were an elderly couple and though I explained to them in great detail whose daughter I was and how we were related through my uncle by marriage, it didn't seem to sink in. But they were very kind and said to me, "Why don't you just come see us and we can figure it out when you get here." By the time I pulled up in front of their apartment, they had figured out who I was and greeted me with open arms.

Lucky for me, they had a cheerful guest room and they said I could take a nice hot bath and change my clothes. Mr. and Mrs. Levinsohn were lovely to me: I ate wonderful home-cooked meals, and that Saturday night they took me to a concert in one of Den-ver's beautiful parks. They took me sightseeing and I still remem-ber Denver as a beautiful city surrounded by majestic mountains.

On Monday morning, I continued my trip on another bus, which would take me to San Francisco in 48 hours. The mountains of Colorado, where we stopped for a fabulous dinner of fresh trout, were absolutely gorgeous. The unique scenery of Utah and Salt Lake City, with the Salt Lake and huge Mormon Cathedral, are etched forever in my memory. We stopped in many small communities to pick up or discharge passengers. I sat next to an American Indian who told me about his life on the reservation. I met a man who lived in the mountains of Colorado, and he told me how people survived during the harsh, cold, snowy winters there. I met school teachers and farmers, and a slow bus ride is just the place to learn about someone's life. People open up to you and their secrets spill out.

We reached Reno in the middle of the night. There were slot machines everywhere, even right there in the bus station and in the restrooms, and people gambled at all hours of the night. I had never been to a casino before and I could not believe my eyes when I saw people gambling in a bus station at 1:00 a.m. in the morning.

The next day, my father's cousin, Eric Gruenfeldt, met me at the bus station in San Francisco. We had not seen each other since I had left Hamburg in October of 1938. Eric was a bachelor and he'd spent a lot of time in our house. I remembered him as a generous uncle who always bought my sister and me the nicest presents; he gave us our first cameras, and one winter he gave us a sleigh.

Eric Gruenfeldt, Margo's father's first cousin

Eric had immigrated to Ecuador, but then settled in San Francisco. His apartment was too small to accommodate a guest, so he had arranged for me to stay with a friend. Eric showed me around and I immediately fell in love with San Francisco. To this day, I still think it is one of the most beautiful cities in the world. Mrs. Goldschmidt, the woman I stayed with, spoiled me, and the two weeks I spent with her and Eric are, indeed, a beautiful memory. After two weeks in San Francisco, I took another bus to Los Angeles and gazed hopefully out of the window at the beautiful scenery along the road as I headed for my new life. I saw oil-drilling fields for the first time in my life, and I also enjoyed the picturesque little towns along the way.

I was going to stay with Herta and Julius who had graciously offered me their home again and told me I could live with them as long as I wanted. They both met me at the bus station, and I was happy to see them. They lived in a lovely apartment in Hollywood, and I would sleep in a Murphy bed in their living room. I had never seen a Murphy bed. I woke up in the middle of the night when my bed started shaking. My first thought was that someone had climbed in through their floor to ceiling windows. I turned on the light. Nobody. I must be having a bad dream, I said to myself. It turned out to be a minor earthquake, another surprising introduction to life in California.

Herta and Julius were wonderful to me. They introduced me to their friends and for a while I worked with them in their business. Then I got a bookkeeping job, which I didn't like very much. Mostly, I didn't like Los Angeles. Everything was so far away. Getting around was not easy. While Herta and Julius were generous and helpful, I was not at all very happy.

It didn't take me very long, however, to realize that I wanted to get back to New York. I was not happy in California.

Margo with Julius and Herta Böninger in California

My oldest and still dearest friend, Uschi, lived nearby, but she was married and had a small baby to take care of. Her husband, Willy, was always happy to pick me up and drive me home again, but he had a strenuous job and I did not want to impose on him too often. Other friends and acquaintances lived too far away; everything is very spread out in California, and without a car it was extremely hard to get around.

I also missed Henry. The only date I went on in L.A. turned out to be a disaster. I was not very receptive to this fellow's advances, and he almost dropped me in the middle of the freeway late in the evening.

For the next eight months, I did little more than muddle through the best I could, and I waited for my chance to return to New York. Lady luck was with me when a neighbor of ours who had a railroad ticket back to New York decided not to go and sold me her ticket. It was still wartime and railroad tickets were very hard to come by. I grabbed that ticket in a heartbeat. I called my parents in Toledo and told them that I was on my way.

I wanted to get back to New York as fast as I could. My mother was very unhappy, assuming that Louis and Vera would settle permanently in California and I would go back to New York. They were also afraid I was going to get back together with Henry, who, up until then, had shown no desire to marry me. My mother was convinced I was going to end up an old maid, and she wasn't afraid to tell me so.

Chapter XXIX
Back in New York

I wrote Henry that I was coming back. It was the mid-1940's, and no one used the phone very much. He promised to find me a temporary place to stay and he said he would pick me up at the railroad station. Indeed, I was very happy to see him. We hugged and kissed. And since he did not own a car yet, we took a taxi to a rather dingy hotel in the West Seventies off Broadway, where Henry had reserved a room for me.

That taxi ride with Henry in New York presented me with a real homecoming. Even Columbus Avenue, which at that time was one of the worst streets on the Westside of Manhattan, seemed beautiful to me because it was familiar. Although Henry made it quite clear that he was not interested in resuming the close relationship we'd had before I went to California, I was happy to be back in New York and to see him.

The next day, I went to see my old bosses on 47th Street. My girlfriend, Lilo, who had taken over my job at Kunstler's, was by now well entrenched with them and I could not get my old job back. However, within a very short time, I found work with a ring manufacturer, Steinmar & Company, who produced rings and sold them to jewelry stores all over the country. It was a very busy place, and my job as the only office employee was very demanding. But I loved it there, and my bosses, Mr. Stein and Mr. Marcus, seemed to be happy with me. All the people working in the factory were very friendly, which made the job even more pleasant. While both bosses took me out for dinner and propositioned me, my refusals did not spoil our good relationship.

In those days, nobody thought of suing anybody for sexual harassment. However, there were always other girls who were willing to have a good time. I learned quite a bit about how so-called happily married men cheated on their wives. "Oh, honey," they would call on the telephone, "I have a late meeting tonight, so don't wait for me with dinner." They did this while some girl was waiting for them in the outer office. It was discreet but still very shocking. My job there ended after two years when they dissolved their business. I'd been very happy to be back on 47th Street, where I knew so many people who seemed to be glad to see me and to talk to me.

It had been difficult to find a place to live in mid-Manhattan. So for a short while, I rented a furnished room from a family on Riverside Drive and 157th Street, in Washington Heights. But I soon found out that I did not like living with a family, nor did I like Washington Heights. I started looking vigorously and found a completely furnished apartment for myself on West 76th Street between Columbus and Amsterdam Avenues, right next to the West Side Institutional Synagogue. The apartment was in one of the many brownstone houses in that area. It was on the ground floor, and although down a few steps, it was not really a basement. There was a rather large living room, a smaller bedroom with a door leading to a nice-sized backyard, a tiny kitchenette, and a bath. Although the furniture was rather dilapidated and the place was not too well-kept, this was my palace. I hired a painter to paint the walls and ceilings, made slipcovers for the chairs and couch, and made bedspreads for my bed. One of my friends who worked at a furniture manufacturer made me a coffee table and two end tables of chrome and black glass. And after buying some inexpensive lamps, the place really looked quite nice. Did I enjoy having a place of my own? Without a doubt! A group of my male friends came over on a weekend to improve the backyard; they turned over the soil, sowed some grass seeds, and planted bushes. After a while, it really looked rather lovely.

It was summer and the services at the synagogue next door were held in their chapel, which was adjacent to my "garden." So on Friday night, I could sit there and listen to the service, and on a Saturday morning, I could even hear it while still lying in bed. All I had to do was open the door of the bedroom. I very much enjoyed listening to the services next door without getting all dressed up.

I spent quite a bit of time with all my girlfriends. We went out to eat, played Mah Jong in each other's apartments, or went to the movies. As far as male company was concerned, I had quite a few dates, mostly with men I met at work. I went to dinners, the movies, and sometimes to the theater or to a concert, but none of these dates developed into anything serious or permanent. Obviously, Henry had not forgotten me and started calling about once a week, and I saw him occasionally. There was still quite a mutual attraction, and after a while we saw each other again on a steadier basis.

My little apartment was quite comfortable, but like so many in Manhattan it also had quite a few unwanted subtenants: roaches and mice. But it's amazing how someone can get used to that. In fact, one little mouse almost became a pet. I had two comfortable chairs in the middle of the room, and after Henry and I started seeing each other again we would often sit there and read. The little mouse would come and stand in front of us on its hind legs like a small dog and would not move for a long time. It was really quite cute, but it was still a mouse! One day, Henry bought spray to get rid of the roaches. He sprayed so much and the odor was so bad that I asked him whether he wanted to kill the roaches or kill me? But it worked. I did not die, but the roaches did, which was a great relief.

Since I had better living quarters than most of my friends, I gave lots of parties. Chianti bottles with candles served as decorations. The standard fare included pretzels and nuts with the drinks, and frankfurters and potato salad for the main dish. Somebody always brought a cake or cookies or another dessert. We danced to the music from a portable record player, and because we were young and enjoyed each other's company we always had a very good time.

The owner of the house, a German woman by the name of Elisabeth Bergman, would occasionally ramble down to the basement and mutter under her breath, "I should throw out the whole bunch of them by their asses." But she never did. Actually, she liked me. She was a scrawny, blonde woman with stringy hair, who drank quite a lot of cheap wine. When not under the influence of alcohol, she would even discuss her shrewd and wise investments with me. I heard that some years later, she sold the house to the synagogue next door for its school and probably made quite a bit of money on it; with this and her investments she could retire very well.

After Steinmar went out of business, I could not find a job on 47th Street, which by now I considered my second home. All the people I knew had bookkeepers and at that time were satisfied with them. Through an ad in *The New York Times*, I found a job with another ring manufacturer, Berman Company, but, unfortunately, it was located on Canal Street in lower Manhattan. Mr. Berman, the owner, was pleasant but strict with his employees. He did not trust them at all and even locked all the supplies in a safe. He would only hand them out after the old ones had become completely unusable. One of the workers said to me, "So he opens the safe, takes out a file, closes the safe, and hands me the file. All this for a cheap file! How ridiculous!"

Fortunately, he trusted me and paid me well, but I was never really happy in that Lower East Side neighborhood. The only redeeming feature was that I was in walking distance of Orchard

Street and all its discount stores. I shopped there during my lunch hour for bargains: underwear, shoes, handbags, suits, linens, towels, and anything and everything else I needed. It was fun shopping there. I worked for Mr. Berman a number of years until I later joined Henry in his business.

PART IV

Chapter XXX

Henry, The Love of My Life

On a cold November afternoon in New York City in 1942, a young refugee from Hitler's Germany, eager to meet other refugees and perhaps to find an old friend enters *La Coupole*, one of the European style coffeehouses on West 72nd Street where many Jewish refugees from Germany and Austria congregated. He glances around the place packed with people chatting, smoking, and drinking coffee.

The tables at *La Coupole* are set very close together, and in between each table stand old-fashioned clothes trees, draped with heavy winter coats and topped with the fedora hats that men in those days wore.

The young man, named Henry, spies a table occupied by a man who has his back to him. He wants to ask the man whether he can join him and share his table. He hangs his hat and coat on the clothes tree and when he does another hat topples down on the man sitting with his back to Henry.

The man twists around to see what is happening and jumps up in astonishment. "My God," he says, "It's Heinz Jungmann! You are here! I cannot believe it is you."

It turns out that the man at the table was my boyfriend Fred.

Heinz Jungmann had by then changed his name to Henry Young ... and as they say in the movies, "The rest is history."

Henry had arrived in New York just a month earlier from France, where he had lived since 1933. Fred and Henry were from the same neighborhood in Berlin and had known each other for a number of years. While they had never been close friends, they'd frequented the same coffee houses and dance bars. But in a new country, however, their common backgrounds made them seem closer. After their chance encounter, Fred asked Henry to make sure to visit him one evening in his furnished room for coffee and cake. "Any way, I want you to meet my girlfriend," Fred told Henry.

Fred's small room was neat and clean, and I set out a cheesecake and made coffee on the little electric burner in the corner; then the doorbell rings.

I don't know whether to really call it "love at first sight." Love has to grow, I think, but there was certainly an instant attraction, almost a chemical attraction that drew Henry and me together. Sometimes, that kind of attraction starts with a look or a spark is ignited by a conversation. Sometimes it's the way a person smiles or the way he moves. Somehow, on that night in 1942, I knew I had met my future husband. Well, maybe I wasn't really conscious of it at the time, but looking back it certainly seems as if Henry and I were drawn together by a force we could not resist.

Henry was at the door, a handsome redhead with sparkling, brown eyes. He was taller than I but not too tall for dancing; he was slim and impeccably dressed. His sport coat was tailor-made, and he had on a long-sleeved shirt with French cuffs and attractive cuff links; his tie was perfectly knotted. He had attended to every detail, and I noticed things like that. His red hair, which was already thinning slightly at 32, was perfectly cut and combed, so that not a hair was out of place.

It was as if a spark had been lit.

A number of things about Henry attracted me: his charm and his intelligence, his good looks and impeccable way of dressing, his good manners, and, of course, the way he talked. But mostly, I think it was the spark that was meant to be ignited by the two of us.

That evening, our conversations were animated. Was there really something between us? Looking back, I am sure that my breaking up with Fred a few weeks later had nothing to do with my having met Henry. I had finally realized that Fred was an incurable, pathological liar, and I could not cope with him any longer. I had been Fred's girlfriend for three years and had stood by him during many trials and tribulations. I even thought I loved him, and at the time I almost married him. Fortunately, I did not.

Of course, I wanted to get married and have children; I knew that. I was twenty-two years old and was looking for an enjoyable and happy future, but Fred was definitely not the man I wanted to spend the rest of my life with. I wonder now if in some subliminal way I knew I was meant for Henry and somehow I set the chain of events in motion. When I broke it off with Fred, he wanted to share his grief with somebody, so the next Sunday morning he visited Henry, who lived with his mother in an apartment on West 81st Street.

Fred told Henry how heartbroken he was that I had left him and how lonely he was. Henry told me later he was absolutely delighted to hear this. He definitely had taken a liking to me, but decent as he was, he would not interfere as long as Fred and I were together.

That same Sunday morning as soon as Fred had left, Henry called up one of his old friends, Claude Levine, and told him that he needed some help, that he had a girl to find! That girl was me. All Henry had to go on was my name and that I lived with some family on West 79th Street between Broadway and Amsterdam Avenue.

And just like in the movies, Henry and Claude went into every building on that block to see if they would find my name together with that of my host family, either on a mailbox or next to a bell. Finally, they hit pay dirt! They found my name together with the name Hirt, in a building on the south side of the street, just a few houses from Amsterdam Avenue. Perseverance had paid off.

In an old-fashioned candy store with telephones and telephone books, Henry excitedly flipped through the directory, then jotted down the address and telephone number on the back of an envelope. He dropped the coins into the phone and called.

I was in the bathtub up to my neck in bubble bath when Lilo Hirt knocked on the door. "There's a Henry Young on the telephone who says he wants to talk to you," she yells through the door.

I jumped out of the bathtub and wrapped myself in a big fluffy towel and ran to the phone. I was about to make my first date with Henry.

On our first date we went to an intimate dance bar on Broadway and 90th Street run by the Kirsch brothers, who had also emigrated from Berlin. They had tried to duplicate the Berlin atmosphere in New York and had pretty much succeeded. There was a small dance floor in the center, and a three-man band played soft, popular dance music. There were comfortable booths along the walls and some tables around the dance floor. The place was dimly lit--but not too dark--and altogether very cozy.

We had a wonderful time on our first evening. We exchanged stories and talked about our backgrounds, which were very similar. We talked about our families and our lives. We danced a little and when Henry took me home, he asked right away for another date, which I was happy to agree to. My friend, Lilo, was still up when I got home, and I remember telling her, "I would like to marry a man like Henry one day."

Margo and Henry

Chapter XXXI
Henry's Past

Henry and I were both born in Hamburg, Germany. His father was one of the top obstetricians and gynecologists in the city, with many wealthy society women among his clientele. Coincidentally, I learned later, my mother had been one of his patients.

Thirty-eight year old Berthold Jungmann was considered charming and good-looking and a very desirable bachelor. A matchmaking relative arranged a meeting with eighteen year old Frieda Suessmann. Frieda was vivacious and intelligent, a raving, red-haired beauty, and she was fascinated by the sophisticated older man.

Having been brought up in a small town in Silesia, the prospect of big city life with its society parties, opera, theaters, and concerts added to the attraction.

When after just a few meetings Berthold asked her to marry him, Frieda was thrilled to accept his proposal.

Frieda's family was rather well-to-do, and they gave her a splendid trousseau: exquisite bed and table linens with hand-embroidered initials; initialed sterling silver flatware sets (I still own one of them); Rosenthal dinner sets and Baccarat glasses; and an elegant new wardrobe of town clothes for her incarnation as a married woman.

After a lavish wedding and the idyllic honeymoon in Italy, Frieda returned to settle into married life in Hamburg. Dr. Jungmann had a large apartment on the second floor of a beautiful building on *Eppendorf Landstrasse 36*, an address which was well known to many of the citizens of the city--not just for the fact that Dr. Jungmann had his practice there... but also because on the first floor of that building was the *Café Nobeling*.

This was no ordinary coffee house, but a quirky, slightly decadent, trysting place for lovers. When you walked in, you entered a long room with booths on either side. Each booth had a pair of heavy damask curtains that drew together for privacy. In order to give the place an air of respectability, an officious man in a morning coat with his hands crossed behind his back would stride up and down the aisle with a bored expression on his face. I suppose the couples smooching behind the curtains in the various booths were mostly discrete, or at minimum remained undiscovered, because I never heard of any serious scandals at the *Café Nobeling*.

Don't get the impression that this part of Eppendorfer was not a fine neighborhood--quite the contrary--*Eppendorf Landstrasse 36* was a well-maintained apartment building, as were the other buildings on the street. The side streets featured old villas, and people of the upper middle class occupied the whole neighborhood.

Dr. Jungmann had both his practice and his living quarters in the same apartment, something quite common then. He had a maid for heavy housework and part-time serving and a full-time housekeeper, who had been with him for many years. This housekeeper and her two children lived in the servant's quarters of the apartment. Gossip had it that Berthold had fathered the housekeeper's two children.

The lack of privacy and the tension between the new bride and the housekeeper must have made it difficult for this 18 year old to establish herself as the mistress of the household. She certainly had new things to deal with. There were the two dachshunds that did not quite know what to think of Frieda and insisted on chewing her beautiful shoes underneath the dining room table while

Frieda and Berthold ate their dinners as man and wife. And there was the hulking German Shepherd who loved Frieda so much that he would jump up and almost topple her over by putting his front paws on her shoulders.

Berthold Jungmann was the son of rich parents who had left him property in a small town in the province of Posen (which is now Poland), where he was born. He had a substantial income from these properties, and the extra money allowed him to live even more comfortably.

This affluence allowed him the luxury of being less than attentive to the business side of his practice, something he'd rather not pay attention to anyway. He was quite careless in billing his patients. Frieda was bright. Both her father and mother were active in their manufacturing business, and she was raised with a good head for business.

Frieda took one look at the mess of unpaid bills and invoices and set out to organize her husband's affairs. She arranged his records and started sending out bills. She quickly found out that some families had never, ever been billed for the delivery and care of their children--and some of these children were already teenagers!

Whether her husband was happy or not with her activities, I do not know, but he was happy with Frieda, and very proud to show off his beautiful young bride to all his friends.

It was said there was some backlash of jealousy from the women who had wanted Dr. Jungmann for themselves, or for their daughters-- some slight shunning. Who knows? Apparently, that didn't affect Frieda. She loved going to the operas, the concerts, the theaters, and the dinner parties to which the young couple was invited. She also loved to entertain. There was plenty of help and plenty of money, and she loved to show off her skills and her beautiful possessions.

Frieda talked to me about all these things later in life, but she never really told me whether she had truly loved Berthold Jungmann. I would have liked to have known this because it might have helped me understand better what eventually happened.

Within a few months after their wedding, Frieda found out that she was pregnant and when her pregnancy began to show, she was told to curtail most of her social activities.

In 1909, pregnant women were not supposed to live their lives filled with happy, social events. They were supposed to disappear, to remove themselves from society.

Being new in Hamburg, she had no good women friends yet, and she was left a great deal by herself—probably with the hostile housekeeper. That friction must have intensified, and all that leisure time unnerved her.

Her very busy physician husband was gone a lot. He was not only a gynecologist but an obstetrician, and babies had a habit of arriving at all times of the day and night.

Berthold's and Frieda's son was born on November 14, 1910. They named him Heinz Max Martin. Heinz was a popular first name in Germany, and his other two names were given in memory of two deceased uncles.

When little Heinz was two months old, Frieda asked her husband for a divorce. She said she could no longer cope with the conditions that surrounded her.

She told me many years later that it was mostly her youth and her inexperience that caused their problems. I still hear her saying, "If I had been twenty-five when I married Berthold, I would have appreciated him more and could have managed all those circumstances much better."

Nevertheless, in 1910, she was only 19 and desperate to get out of the marriage. Berthold, however, did not want this. He refused to give her the divorce. He said he didn't want to lose her or his baby son.

Frieda was desperate, and she planned an escape. Somehow or other, Berthold found out the exact date on which Frieda was planning to run off. He got help from a government official who said he would come and physically prevent Frieda from taking the baby.

But she got wind of this. When she saw the man actually come up the stairs, she panicked and threw her fur muff into his face, temporarily blinding him.

She grabbed her baby and ran wildly down the stairs into a waiting taxi and tore off to hide out with an uncle who lived in another part of Hamburg. I was always amazed at her guts, a young nineteen year old leaving everything to take off alone with her little boy.

After a long struggle, Berthold finally gave in and gave her the divorce. Frieda had moved to Berlin with Heinz, and four years later, when the First World War broke out, they moved back to *Liegnitz*, in Silesia, to be with her parents, who were overjoyed to have their first grandchild with them. Little Heinz was brought up as if he was the youngest child in the family, since his mother's younger sister, Edith, was only 12 years older than he was.

When Heinz was old enough to inquire about his father, everyone told him that his father had died when he was an infant.

I guess Frieda thought she was doing the right thing. However, when he was 13, Heinz somehow found out that his father was alive and well, and he insisted on meeting him.

Berthold had remained unmarried; at almost 50, he was still in practice at *Eppendorfer Landstrasse 36*.

That was where Heinz found him, where he was reunited with his overjoyed father.

After that, Heinz visited Berthold very often, and a great bond formed between them; his father instilled in him a solid interest in medicine.

Frieda Scheyer, Henry's Mother

I guess I should be happy that things turned out the way they did, or I wouldn't have met Heinz/Henry, but if circumstances had not prevented him from doing so, my husband would have no doubt become a doctor in Germany, and taken over his father's practice.

Poor dear Father Jungmann died in the concentration camp *Theresienstadt*, allegedly of natural causes at the age of 73.

Chapter XXXII
Mrs. Young

Henry hadn't actually proposed to me, but we'd discussed the possibility of getting married if we could find a suitable apartment. Apartments were still hard to find, even a few years after the end of the war, and Henry definitely did not want to start married life in my apartment on 76th Street. He wanted to move into a nice building with new furniture and modern appliances. So did I.

I met Anne and Eric Weil at a summer resort, and they told me that they lived in a new development in Queens called *Fresh Meadows*. "It is really beautiful," they told me, "and we love it there."

"Are there any apartments available?" I asked. "I am going with a fellow who would marry me if we found a suitable apartment."

Anne said, "Well, they are still building new garden apartments and when I get home I will find out." Henry did not want to stay in Manhattan anyway. He had told me repeatedly that he wanted to see green trees and lawns when he came home from the office. I hoped that Anne would keep her word and that we would find an apartment there.

Henry arrived at the hotel shortly after lunch on Friday. Eric had just left the dining room and was standing outside when Henry got out of his car. When they saw each other, they embraced. They had been good friends in Paris, but they'd lost touch during the war. They were absolutely elated to see each other and they immediately started talking about their lives since they last saw each other. After a while, Henry said to Eric, "You know, I really think I should look for my girl before we continue talking."

Eric asked, "You aren't by any chance Margo Shrag's boyfriend?"

Henry was baffled and Eric explained how we'd met. The four of us had a great weekend together, and we promised to get together again when we returned to New York. We were eager to visit them out in Fresh Meadows.

They had a lovely two-bedroom apartment they'd taken when Anne got pregnant. They showed us all around, and we liked the place; it was beautifully landscaped. In addition to the high rises where Eric and Anne lived, there were some two- and three-story garden-type apartments, and more were under construction.

There was an A & P Supermarket and a Bloomingdale's department store close by and a gas station right at the entrance to the Fresh Meadows development. The main access street was Horace Harding Boulevard, which is now the Long Island Expressway. Everything looked great--we told the Weils that we were very interested and to please let us know if and when anything opened up.

One afternoon in December, Anne called me at the office and said, "Margo, come out right away. I just learned they are building a new section of garden apartments and if you want one, you've got to come and fill out the application today."

I hopped on the subway to Flushing and then took a bus to Fresh Meadows.

Anne went with me to the office to introduce me to the apartment manager. The new section would be ready in March of the following year. They showed me a model apartment, which I loved: a nice-sized living room with an L-shaped dining area, an adequate bedroom, a small kitchen, which had a space in front of a window for a table and two chairs, and a bathroom. Everything was new and modern, and I was terribly excited about how wonderful it would be to start my married life in one of these apartments. I filled out the application, and then the lady said, "Everything looks okay, but we need your fiancé's signature before we close today at 9:00 p.m."

I called Henry and he promised to meet me at the Weil's apartment as soon as he could get there.

I can still see the two of us: Anne, who was very pregnant by then, and me, walking through the snow back to their apartment. We were talking and planning when finally the doorbell rang.

Anne said, "It must be Henry, you open it."

I can picture the scene in front of me vividly: Henry outside and me inside the entry door, facing him.

Henry said, "Do you really want to marry me?"

I threw my arms around him and said, "That was a proposal, wasn't it?"

Then I added, "But shouldn't I *think* about this before rushing into anything?"

Henry laughed and we went to the office so he could sign the application.

On April 10, 1949, we got married in the studio of Rabbi Hahn's apartment on Fort Washington Avenue, in Washington Heights. Rabbi Hahn was from Essen, Germany and he was the first Rabbi of Congregation Habonim, which I had joined many years before.

We did not have a "chuppa," but the rabbi draped a talis around both our shoulders. Henry was perspiring and a little shaky. I had the feeling that he was still not quite sure if he was doing the right thing. He looked extremely handsome in his navy suit with white pin stripes. I wore a navy blue suit with a white blouse, a little white hat with a veil, and navy blue platform shoes with very high heels (which Henry loved). He had brought a corsage of white roses for me, which I still have, dried and preserved. I haven't the faintest idea what the rabbi said to us, but it didn't matter at all. I was so happy that I was finally married to the man I loved and adored, and I hoped that the marriage would last.

In some ways I was very doubtful. I actually told a few of my friends that I thought it would only last a year or perhaps two. I was afraid that two very strong willed people would collide and we would not be able to make a go of it.

But it turned out to be a wonderful marriage based on mutual love, respect, and understanding for each other. It lasted forty-four and a half years until Henry's death on October 10, 1993.

Henry's mother gave us a lovely wedding dinner at her apartment. She hired a woman to cook and serve. There were ten of us. The table was beautifully set, the dinner was delicious, the spirit festive, and there was a real wedding cake with a bridal couple made of clay on the top, which I also still have.

Unfortunately, my family was missing. My mother was still recuperating from surgery, and my father did not want to leave her. My sister was pregnant with her second child and had a small infant at home.

Henry and Margo on their wedding day, April 10, 1949

It was strange not having anyone from my family at the wedding to share in my happiness.

After dinner, we drove to Fresh Meadows to our new apartment, which was completely bare of furniture, except for the mattresses. Did we really need anything else for a wedding night? We certainly didn't, and were happy to have each other.

We never went on a honeymoon, although I did take off a week from my job. I wanted to fix up the apartment as much as I could.

The day before the wedding, I'd waited at the apartment all day for the mattresses to come. I was worried we wouldn't have a bed on our wedding night! The truck was late, and I'd paced back and forth, fiddling ... lining the kitchen and closet shelves and doing little odds and ends, sitting in the empty apartment on the only thing to sit on ... the toilet seat!

We could hardly wait for the new furniture to come. Our bedroom set was being made for us out of ebony wood, and the rest of our furniture had been ordered. Our friend, the interior decorator Henry Nesselroth, had ordered beautiful modern furnishings for us, and I was lucky: all the furniture arrived the week I was home; when everything was put in its place, the apartment looked beautiful.

A snappy red circular couch and a comfortable green armchair were set off by the draw drapes that had the same complementary colors in a modern print. All the wood pieces were made of shiny, dark brown mahogany. There was a kidney-shaped glass coffee table, modern floor lamps, and a streamlined chandelier over the dining room table. The kitchen had a small table and two chairs in front of its window, where we could eat breakfast or lunch, but I would only serve dinner on the dining room table. I went to the supermarket, which was just a block away, and stocked my little kitchen. I cooked dinner for the two of us, and we enjoyed being together in our apartment with our beautiful new furniture, especially after all the years we'd spent in furnished rooms.

Margo and Henry in their new home in Fresh Meadows, NY, 1949

I went back to work the following week. It was a long trip. I first had to take a bus on Horace Harding Boulevard. The bus took me to the Flushing Station of the IRT Subway.

On 34th Street, I had to change to the IND to Canal Street, and from there it was a few short blocks to my office. I did not mind it at all. Although it was usually around 6:30 in the evening when I got home, I would set a nice table and cook a full course dinner for the two of us. Henry liked soup, or an appetizer, meat or fish with vegetables and potatoes, plus dessert and coffee. I wasn't a great cook then, but with the help of my mother's cookbook and the advice of my mother-in-law, I managed quite well. Later on, our friend Fred List, who was a chef by profession, taught me much, much more, and I must say that I became quite a good cook. Even then, I loved cooking and trying out new recipes, and if Henry was pleased I glowed with pride.

Henry felt that he could expand his business by taking a trip to the Far East. One evening, he asked me, "Would you consider quitting your job and joining my business to supervise the office? I really don't trust Mrs. Lewinson (his only employee) to run the office properly while I'm gone."

I was very reluctant at first. Henry wanted perfection, and he had a tendency to get very upset if things were not done exactly how he wanted them. A husband and wife working together could be disastrous, and the last thing I wanted to do was ruin our marriage. I had waited long enough already to be married and I did not want to mess things up, but Henry begged me and I said I would give it a try.

He promised to be back in three weeks, but the trip stretched out to almost three months. That was hard on a new bride. From the Far East, he had to go to Jerusalem because his uncle who lived there was sick and he wanted to see him. In the meantime, some business opportunities also had opened up in Ireland, and Henry felt they were worth investigating. Of course, we stayed in touch, but our communications were limited to telephone calls, telegrams, and letters, which always took a very long time to arrive. There were no computers or fax machines, of course. I managed to keep the business running, but it was not easy.

The secretary, who was in her mid to late fifties, resented my taking charge. But Henry had been right. She was not meticulous enough. Export shipping documents had to be flawless in order to collect against a Letter of Credit. I discovered a few mistakes, which she corrected, but it always put her into a snit. I was on the verge of firing her several times, but I was not the boss and I felt I had no right to do it. When Henry came back, I said, "I almost fired your secretary," and he said, "I wish you had. It would have spared me the unpleasant job."

During that time, I also learned to drive. I had taken driving lessons while I was still working on Canal Street, and later on I told everybody that anyone learning to drive between the baby buggies and trucks of the Lower East Side could master driving any place.

Margo driving

My teacher thought I was doing quite well and after a few lessons he told me to go home and practice with my husband during the weekend. Bad advice! Henry had no patience and, as always, wanted perfection. One Sunday morning Henry said to me, "Let me see if you can make a proper U-turn."

Our streets in Fresh Meadows were not very wide, and we still drove a standard shift car. As always, I thought I could master anything, but I backed our brand new Plymouth into a fire hydrant and ruined the trunk. I don't have to describe what followed, but I continued with my lessons and finally got my license. After the trunk episode, Henry wouldn't let me drive when he was in the car.

When Henry was away, I practiced by myself and got some friends to help me. I learned to drive just fine. I would always accompany Henry to the airport and drive the car home, and when he came back I would pick him up. Of course, he would be the one behind the wheel when we drove home.

He never let me drive him again until years later when he suffered a mild heart attack and was not allowed to drive for three months. One day, I was driving him and he said to me, "You know, you really have become a good driver." After that, he never minded when I took the wheel.

Henry fired his secretary, hired a new, younger one, and I stayed on. He traveled a lot, and it was always good to have him home again. After I picked him up at the airport, we would sit in our comfortable living room and he would tell me all about his accomplishments and escapades. Why not? We were husband and wife and best friends and, after a while, business partners as well. I had decided that I wanted to help Henry build up his business, instead of working for somebody else, and, as it turned out, we got along extremely well.

We were exporting a variety of products to multiple markets, as there was a shortage of many items around the world in the years after World War II. Before long, I was very much involved in all aspects and activities of the business. We were receiving inquiries for many different kinds of merchandise, from textiles to air conditioning pipes. Henry would hand me the inquiries and my job would be to find manufacturers who made these items. We had huge books called "THOMAS" Directories, which listed manufacturers of every conceivable product. How much easier it is today with computers! It was not always easy finding the right source for a given product. There were technical items with specifications, which I did not understand, and there were metric figures that had to be converted. But I managed. Sometimes, the manufacturers would take the time to explain the specifications to me. All in all, it was interesting and fun, and I learned a lot and was very proud when I came up with a proper offer for a required item.

Our main customer was a large, established import firm in Sweden. After a while, the manager came to New York for a visit. He was a charming man who spoke English and German fluently. We invited him to our home for dinner and to our favorite French restaurant. He was an opera lover, and we took him to the Metropolitan Opera on 40th Street and Broadway, with tickets in the Grand Tier.

Henry and I would have loved to have had children, but I could not seem to get pregnant. Fertility pills did not exist at that time, and we definitely did not want to adopt. We had witnessed three cases where the adopted children, in spite of all their parents' efforts, became problems. Of course, we knew that could happen with your own children too, but we felt adoption would pose a greater risk.

And then, in February of 1953, my mother died. I had a sneaking suspicion that I might be pregnant, but I had not yet gone to the doctor. When I came back from the funeral, I had a miscarriage--probably caused by the shock and strain--and I never became pregnant again.

My mother's death hit me very hard. She was only 54, looked so much younger than her years, and was so full of life. She and Daddy had just sold their house and had moved to a lovely, modern apartment. She hadn't been feeling well, her stomach was bothering her, and she had no appetite. As was her habit, she had waited to see a doctor until her condition became very bad. When she was admitted to the hospital, they found that she had developed adhesions from the colon operation. A surgeon told my family he felt she was too weak to survive an operation.

They waited and she died of peritonitis, which I felt then, and still feel today, was the result of gross negligence. At least, they should have tried to operate--they might have saved her.

Henry was my tower of strength. When we heard the bad news, he immediately ordered sleeper tickets on a train leaving the same night. He had his arms around me and tried to console me, but it was so hard to lose my mother, especially at such a young age. And my poor father was completely broken up. They had such an exceptionally happy marriage, which for 30 years had lasted through all their hardships; for my father, facing life alone was hard. There was also my sister, with her two small children, ages two and four. Vera had leaned so much on our mother for help and for advice, and now she was on her own. The memory of our beloved mother is still very much with us, and whenever my sister and I get together, we still recall what Mutti would have said or done in this or in that situation.

After staying another week with my dad, I went back to New York to be with my Henry and to take care of my job in our business.

Chapter XXXIII
Paris

I would finally see Paris. I'd never been to Paris--Henry's Paris--but it was his second hometown, and he knew it so well. I was about to see the city Henry had shared with me through stories and memories. Only this time, we would see Paris together.

Henry told the taxi driver exactly how to get to our hotel. "Avoid the Champs-Élysées," he told the driver.

"Why did you want to *avoid* the Champs-Élysées?" I asked. I, of course, was anxious to see everything, including that famous boulevard.

"I'll tell you later," he said, as we arrived at the Hotel Intercontinental on the Rue de Rivoli, a beautiful building with an indoor covered garden. We were practically across the street from the Louvre. Our room, on an upper floor, looked out on the roofs of Paris and my head filled with the song "Sur les Toit de Paris." The room had old world brass beds, beautiful duvets, and comfortable chairs. We unpacked and took a nap. Then as the lights on the streets below came on, Henry said, "It's time to get ready. Now I want to show you Paris."

We walked out of the hotel, and a few short blocks later we stopped and Henry said, "Now look." There in front of me was, indeed, the Champs-Élysées rising toward the spectacularly illuminated Arc de Triomphe.

I turned to Henry, my eyes shining. I kissed him and thanked him for showing me Paris. He said, "This is how I wanted to show you the Arc de Triomphe. I didn't want you to see it any other way, at night, illuminated, with me. You will never forget this view. Isn't it magnificent?"

How right he was; it was soul stirring and impressive, and I have never forgotten it. What a shame that years later fast food restaurants like Burger King, Kentucky Fried Chicken, and other chain and discount stores have spoiled the feeling of the area!

That evening, we walked all the way to the impressive monument built in the middle of the Place d'Etoile with 12 of Paris' major avenues radiating into the center. There, underneath it imbedded into the ground, was the Tomb of the Unknown Soldier with its perpetual flame. All these many years later, I still vividly see the whole scene in my memory.

We were getting hungry and Henry took me to one of his favorite restaurants on the Champs-Élysées. We walked down a few steps and into a small, cozy restaurant with comfy banquettes along the wall. The food was delicious, and we shared a bottle of wonderful Bordeaux.

The next day was the 14th of July, Bastille Day, France's national holiday, and we went across the street from the hotel to the Tuileries Gardens, where we could see the festive parade. Henry helped me climb up on a bench so I could see better. There I was with all these cheering Parisians, watching their thrilling parade: the distinctive military regiments and the French Foreign Legion in their colorful uniforms. Formations of airplanes flew overhead trailing red, white, and blue flag-colored smoke streams. I got gooseflesh and became damp-eyed when the band music played. Henry told me I looked just like a little kid.

Henry took me up to Montmartre that evening. For some reason, he insisted we take the Metro, the Paris subway. "Why can't we take a bus or taxi?" I said. "I'd like to see the city, not be stuck underground." Henry obviously had his reasons, so I didn't mention it again.

When we got out of the subway, Henry walked me uphill along cobblestone streets. I had a hard time in my tight skirt and high heels. All of a sudden, Henry stopped and told me, "Turn around."

What I saw was a *boulangerie*, a bakery, in front of me and then the landmark la *Basilique du Sacre Coeur de Montmartre*, the Basillica of the Sacred Heart, which sits on the highest point in Paris.

I said to Henry, "How beautiful, but it's strange. I've never been to Paris but this all looks so familiar to me. What is it, deja vu? Could I have dreamed this?" Henry just stood there smiling and said, "Look again, and think...."

Painting of Montmartre

Then, it dawned on me. Henry's mother had given us a painting of the same exact view. I couldn't get over the fact that Henry had gone to all this trouble to take me to the precise spot where the painter had stood.

We then slowly walked all the way up Montmartre butte, to the *Place du Tertre*, through narrow and winding cobblestone streets lined with very old houses. On reaching the front of the *Basilique du Sacre Coeur*, we beheld a most spectacular view of Paris at eventide.

We went to one of the very lovely restaurants on the square and enjoyed the delicious and exotic fish they served, much different from the fish we were used to in the United States. By the time we finished, it was dark, and we walked back to where we had seen all of Paris in the twilight. Now the city was alive below us with nighttime energy and bright lights. The special holiday fireworks exploded and shot skyward from every direction. Paris was alight in a splendid, celebratory show.

We walked down to the *Place de Fuerstenberg*, a charming, little square surrounded with old houses. One of Henry's Parisian girlfriends had lived there, and our stroll must have brought back fond memories.

Our next stop was Rue Jacob. It was a beautiful warm summer night, and from the open doors of many restaurants and bars we could hear live music. Henry had told me that on the 14th of July people actually danced in the streets, and, lo and behold, here we were on this charming street, and couples were, indeed, drifting outside to dance. It was Bastille Day in Paris and it doesn't get much more historic or more romantic than this. And I couldn't thank Henry enough for bringing me here.

The next day, we went to the Louvre. We made a point to see the Mona Lisa and her smiling gaze that seems to follow you no matter where you stand. Dozens of art students had set up their easels around the painting, and they were doing their best to copy it. I thought they were awfully optimistic considering the master-work they were attempting to replicate. But I applauded them for trying. The Louvre was once a palace, and the museum's interior, its marble stairs, and ornate decorations, add to the astonishing, somewhat overwhelming richness of the atmosphere. There was entirely too much to assimilate, and I came away with my head filled with fantastical images.

That evening, we went to bed early and set the alarm for 1:00 a.m. Henry wanted to show me *Les Halles* where he'd had his wholesale fruit business when he lived in Paris before the war.

Henry and his partner were actually the first to introduce grape-fruits into the Parisian market. The grapefruits came from Palestine (now Israel), where his partner from Berlin had settled and where he'd married the daughter of a man who owned orange and grapefruit plantations. *Les Halles* was the famous old fruit and vegetable whole-sale market, and it bustles with energy all through the night.

Nowadays, it is in a different location, but when we were there in 1960, everything was more or less the same as it was during the time before the war when Henry and his partner had their business there.

Henry pointed out their exact location amid the chaos of the wonderful show. Everything was so picturesque, the aromas of the melons and fruits so tantalizing, the market a circus of vendors and customers and their stalls. We walked around for a long time that night. Henry found a few people he'd known, and he had great fun telling me all sorts of tales. Finally, we got hungry.

Henry knew where there were a few informal restaurants for the workers and customers. In the typical French tradition, only the freshest seasonal ingredients were used in this simple, straight-forward cooking.

You can't believe how, in the middle of the night like that, how marvelous a bowl of perfectly prepared onion soup can taste-- I doubt any has ever been so memorable to me. Looking over that rustic table at Henry that night I knew the meaning of true love.

Chapter XXXIV
Our Business

"**I**f you've already had your own business, you will want to go back to it and be on your own," Henry's boss had told him. He knew Henry would stay only long enough to earn start-up money to go back into business for himself. He was right as rain.

Henry wanted to make the profits for himself, instead of making them for someone else, and he wanted to build up a business for his future. First, he rented a desk in an office on 42nd Street and contacted some overseas importing firms he was familiar with. It was less than a year after the end of World War II, and the whole world needed all kinds of merchandise, which was very often very hard to get. A Swedish firm became Henry's first good customer.

This was before Henry and I got married. He was still living with his mother, and I had my apartment on West 75th Street. His sister had not arrived from Israel yet, and we were seeing each other on a regular basis.

On weekends, Henry and I would sit in his room with two typewriters and write letters to companies around the world offering the services of HENRY M. YOUNG, INC., hoping to acquire any type of merchandise for them. Soon Henry was able to move his office from desk space to a private room, which he sublet from a very nice man by the name of Jack Taylor. The office was on the second floor of a walk-up building on the corner of Eighth and 40th Streets, right across from New York City's main bus terminal.

While it was not the best neighborhood, the office was bright and cheerful and there was maid service. There were two desks, one for Henry and one for a secretary, plus space for files and filing cabinets. Henry was happy and so was I.

He told me all the details about the emerging business, and I did some bookkeeping for him on the side. It became more and more interesting. The main part of our business was still focused on exporting a variety of different items, but we were now also producing fabrics for umbrellas, the bulk of which we exported to the Philippines.

Henry was an experienced and inventive businessman; when he found a market, he pounced on the opportunity. Why was there such a demand for umbrella fabrics in the Philippines? Because most Philippine women (and some men) use umbrellas to protect themselves against the strong sun.

Henry found contractors who could weave and print these fabrics for us. He went to the Philippines with his first collection, found a sales agent, George Salman, and immediately sold large quantities to the four Chinese umbrella manufacturers in Manila that provided the Philippine market with their finished products.

On one of his trips, Henry made a home movie while attending a bullfight in Manila. Throughout the arena, you can see all the people with their umbrellas made from our fabrics. People in the Philippines preferred wild and funny designs. The basic colors were usually green, blue, and burgundy, but the borders were often in rainbow colors. We printed fabrics with designs of monkeys and parrots, fruits and vegetables, and all kinds of other exotic images. It was great fun to consult the design books and come up with each new collection. I became quite experienced in making new designs that could be adapted to our fabrics.

Henry found the weaving contractors and printing companies and arranged for the production. I became the go between, the coordinator. Every day, I phoned suppliers to make sure our deliveries would be on time. I visited the printers to oversee that the correct designs were printed on the proper fabrics.

It was both fun and frustrating: we would urgently need some green fabric, but the mill might be in the middle of weaving blue; or we needed a certain print to complete an order, but the printer had just started working on a new run for a different customer.

I kept very busy pleading and placating, figuring out how to keep the customers happy, and I loved it. Henry was preoccupied with shipping companies and finding the best deals. In those days, everything went by freighter and took a long time to reach the Philippines, and sometimes storms or strikes caused additional headaches and delays.

We were now making money, but a side benefit for Henry, a reward of sorts, was the great time he had on his semi-annual working vacations to Manila. At that time--the days of the propeller planes--a trip that far away had many stops. First, he traveled to the West Coast, then to Hawaii with a couple of days at the very best hotel at that time, the *Royal Hawaiian Hotel,* then the flight over the Pacific. Henry flew in the first-class section with sleeper compartments, much like railroad Pullman cars.

Passengers were greeted by name, attentively pampered, and by today's standards, they were treated like royalty. There were stops in either Guam or the Midway Islands for refueling before the plane landed in Manila. George, our agent, would greet Henry with a sign in one hand and a bottle of Scotch in the other.

Henry stayed at the *Manila Hotel,* right in the center of the city. While he worked hard during the day visiting the various umbrella manufacturers to secure contracts, evening was party time. Although Henry was the supplier, our customers were so happy to see him that each one gave him a party. There were drinking parties at either the customers' homes or in restaurants. Our customers were all Chinese, and wives never attended these functions. Very often, "party girls" were invited. How do I know all this? Henry told me.

A party in Manila, 1950

One evening, it got somewhat out of hand when all these grown-up men threw glasses filled with liquor through the open windows of a second floor restaurant onto the plaza below. The police took the whole bunch of them to the police station, including Henry, George, the Chinese customers, and the girls. On the way to the station, pie-eyed George, from the back of the paddy wagon, tried to tell the police officer the best way to drive to jail.

At the police station, the inebriated Chinese started to sing the Chinese national anthem, which struck everybody as very, very funny. After they had sobered up a little, everyone was released and everyone went home happy and hung-over.

Henry always came home with big orders, which kept our looms running for quite a while, until George booked even more business. George, who was born in Nazareth, Palestine, and his wife, Eli, who was a Philippina, visited us in New York one year. I found them both to be lovely people and easy to get along with. One day, during their visit, George remarked to Henry, "You are so fortunate to have married your own kind."

"Why?" Henry replied. "Aren't you happy with Eli and the five children she's given you?"

"Yes," George said. "Actually, I am not unhappy, but there is a drastic difference in our upbringing and in our cultures. Some in her family still eat food with their fingers! And, of course, there are many other things.... All I can say is that you are a very lucky man."

Henry understood what he meant; coming from the same kind of German-Jewish, upper middle class family, Henry and I understood each other and found comfort in our common culture and traditions.

Over time, the Philippines tried to become more and more independent from United States domination; they became an independent republic on July 4, 1946, but there were certain military and trade agreements that still bound them to the United States. While we continued to sell umbrella goods there, the government instituted certain quotas on textiles, which affected us greatly. During his many visits there, Henry had established a good relationship with some of the Philippine senators, even making a speech to the Philippine Senate, trying to explain to them that the new quotas would hurt the Philippine economy more than it would help. But no one was listening. Japan began offering fabrics cheaper than ours, and after a while our business with the Philippines came to an end.

Chapter XXXV
The Import Business

W e made a drastic change to our business. We decided to switch from exporting to importing. Our first advertisement resulted in a strange request. We were contacted by a company that wanted to buy *barbed elastics*. What exactly were those? We definitely wanted to know. We eventually learned a lot about these thin elastic cords with barbed point ends.

Before molded plastic was used to hold things to cardboard cards for hanging displays, items were attached with thin, white elastic cords with little metal barbs crimped on the ends. The pointy end of each silvery barb went through a pre-punched tiny hole in the card, and the barb was pulled through and twisted flat against the back of the card, so that the cord wouldn't slip back through the hole, thus securing the object to the card. Usually, two or three elastics were used on each item to hold it fast.

A small factory owner in Manhattan who we had known for a while said he wanted to find these products at a price cheaper than they would cost if he manufactured them himself. Henry was clever, and he im-

Henry in Japan, 1951

mediately saw it as a business opportunity. He took movie pictures of the man's factory, the machines, and the workers during the production process. He went to Japan with his footage, and found a bilingual agent named Bill Connor.

Bill had served in the American Army in Japan and liked it so well that he stayed there after the end of the war. He and Henry found a small Japanese manufacturer, showed them the film and the samples, and set up production of barbed elastics.

That was our start, and soon many other products followed. Henry was ambitious, creative, and hard-working. He made many trips to Japan and Hong Kong to look for suitable items to import. While the trips were certainly long, they were always enjoyable for him, although I'd like to believe he missed me a little.... At least, he was smart enough to tell me so.

Henry discovered that there was a market for narrow elastic webbing used in the manufacture of men's suspenders. For a while, suspenders were a popular fashion item. They were also worn by workers to hold up their pants because they were more comfortable--and cheaper--than belts. Henry found weaving mills in Japan that produced these elastic webbings cheaper than any United States' producers did. It became a good business because there were quite a number of suspender manufacturers in the United States who produced sizable quantities.

At first, Henry serviced these customers, but since he was traveling so much to find new sources and supervise the established ones, I began to take over the sales part of our business. I loved it.

I made up sample cards of our various products and started out visiting suspender manufacturers in New York City. The customers liked our merchandise, and they liked me. Because of that, our products sold very well.

First, we sold suspender elastics from Japan, but later on we got them from better, more competitive sources in Italy. You always had to be one step ahead. One thing led to another, and soon we were importing elastics from Germany that we sold to brassiere manufacturers.

By this time, Henry had acquired some well known name-brand manufacturers as customers. While he personally sold to these customers, I came up with the bright idea that I could expand the business if I helped with the bra sales. I knew there were many brassière manufacturers out there besides the ones we already sold to so I said to my husband, "Let me see if I can drum up some additional business and some new customers."

"Sure," he said. "See what you can do."

Before I started, I became familiar with all the technical things I needed to know. I learned about the various widths we could manufacture and the specific prices. I learned how to pitch my products by giving potential customers my assurance that our products were all colorfast, that the hottest water even commercial laundries used wouldn't ruin the stretch in our elastics, and that we, in the end, were offering the perfect elastic for brassieres at a better price than anyone else. Armed with this information, I took my sample case and went to Madison Avenue.

Any New Yorker knows how special industries are confined to certain sections of the city. The offices and showrooms of the brassière and corset industry were on Madison Avenue between 30th and 34th Street. That's where I went: from one building to the next, from one floor to the other to solicit business. On my initial visits to the showrooms, I was told that buyers would only see vendors on certain days of the week, usually early in the morning.

I kept a list and made up a precise schedule. It was quite an experience for me to walk into the waiting rooms of these prospective buyers and see fifteen or twenty men glaring at me with unfriendly faces. They had never seen a young woman on their turf, and I was told that they thought that a woman with all her charm would constitute unfair competition. However, on first meeting me, the buyers usually greeted me warmly but with condescension.

But it didn't take a mind reader to figure out they liked seeing a "cute broad" for a change, so I was extremely careful to conduct my sales appointments in a high-toned, business like manner.

When I opened my sample case and went into my spiel, explaining the technical details of the various webbings, they looked at me differently. I got their attention and respect, and some became my good customers.

I thought eventually things would change and I would be accepted, but things didn't change and I was never fully accepted; each time I went to one of the showrooms, it was like walking into a hornet's nest. My competitors never got any friendlier. By then I had become a regular salesperson trespassing on their territory, and none of these guys wanted a woman as a competitor, especially a woman offering a superior product at a fair price. Nobody ever spoke to me unkindly or said anything specifically, but their unfriendly looks said they'd prefer to run me out of town.

Our business kept developing, however. Henry found that in some European countries certain linens, fancy velvets, and velveteen were being produced cheaper and better than here in America.

He located large textile producers who were willing to buy these items from us. Our German manufacturer, who produced the brassière elastics, also sent us beautiful fancy elastics that were very much in demand in the shoe industry.

I did some research and learned that there were three or four shoe supply wholesalers in the New York area. Two of them immediately became very good customers, and apparently word got around the trade that an attractive, young woman was selling these items, items which would soon be essential in leisure footwear.

At first, the production at our German mill was limited, but when they saw that more and more orders were coming in, they increased production and I went about trying to find more customers.

I will never forget the day I called a shoe supply wholesaler in Brooklyn to try to set up an appointment. I got the owner on the phone. His first words were, "Are you the little blonde woman going around the city selling elastics? Because if you are, I've heard you have some very nice stuff. I've been looking for you, but nobody would give me your number. Will you come out to see me?" Being a woman in a man's world sometimes had its advantages. That fellow became an excellent customer.

We also noticed that men's belts were being made out of webbing instead of leather. Our German mill did not produce the type of webbing that we needed in our market, so we searched for suppliers in other countries. Now *that* was tedious work. I had to go to the commercial section of the various foreign consulates and review their reference books. I scoured the huge volumes of trade books to find manufacturers that might possibly produce the right items for us. After identifying a few names, one of our secretaries would send out letters and inquiries. Then, it was a matter of waiting for their replies.

Working as a woman in a man's world was a great experience. Henry was now depending on me to service my accounts. I took my work seriously, and together we were developing a fine, solid business. I had earned the respect of my customers and they valued my opinion. We were selling fashion items, and I had to be up-to-date with the colors and designs that became popular for each season.

I went to trade shows and read fashion magazines to make sure I had my finger on the fashion pulse. My customers depended on me to know what I was talking about, and I could not afford to miss a trend or make a style mistake that would lose money for them. That would have been the end of my hard-won personal success, and both Henry and I were working too hard to have that happen.

Chapter XXXVI

The Unforgettable Mr. Liebaert

W hen the Japanese mills could no longer make the belt webbing we wanted, we found a manufacturer in Belgium who could, the firm of Marcel Liebaert.

We first met Henri Liebaert, himself, in the summer of 1960 in our hotel in Brussels, Belgium. By then, we were buying considerable quantities of belt elastic from his mill, located outside of Brussels in the small town of Deinze. We were eager to meet Henri, and to see how they made the material we were importing.

Henri Liebaert met us in the lobby of our hotel one evening at around six. About 65, he was an imposing, round faced man, tall and heavy, with thinning gray hair and piercing eyes.

Liebaert spoke fluent English. We ordered drinks and he started telling us about his family's roots in Belgium, in Ghent. "I call it the 'old firm.'" he said to us. "After all, it was founded by my grandfather."

It had passed down from father to son, then father to son again, and eventually Henri's two sons would take over when he retired. After graduating from the university, Henri was sent to Krefeld, in Germany, one of the cities in Europe that produced high-class textiles. He worked for a while as a so-called "volunteer," meaning without pay, and learned all the intricacies of textile production. He took special courses at the Krefeld Textile Institute and learned to speak fluent German. "Children," as he called Henry and me, "am I boring you with all these details?"

"Oh, no!" we said "Tell us more. We really would like to learn." We ordered more drinks.

"My brother and I were in the business together. We made knitted fabrics and elastics and the business was doing well, but I wanted very much to get into politics. I did. I got elected to the Belgian Senate, and I left the 'old firm.'"

It was quite an honor," he said, "I was presented to King Leopold wearing striped trousers, a morning coat, and a top hat."

Henri Liebaert was basking in his memories. He was a man capable of anything, and a number of years later he was appointed Secretary of Finance.

At this point, Henri Liebaert stopped his storytelling and said, "Now we have to decide where to eat, don't you think? We have elegant places in Brussels, but there is one restaurant I like best, not too fancy but they have terrific food." The little store-front restaurant that we dined at had eight or ten tables and was called *Comme Chez Soi*, meaning *Like at Home*. It has since become world famous and has been written up in many gourmet and travel magazines.

The owner welcomed Henri as "Votre Excellence," a title used for dignitaries. Dinner was outstanding. The chef came out during the soup course with a platter displaying a variety of raw fish, and we discussed the fish we wanted and how he would prepare it. We did the same for the meat course. Everything was superb, including the wines and the fabulous desserts at the end of dinner.

While we were eating, my husband asked Henri Liebaert why he returned to the world of business. "What made you come back to the family business after holding such a prestigious government office?" Henry asked.

"Well," Henri Liebaert said, "it was a difficult decision. Sad to say, I did not think my brother was running the business well enough. I was afraid that if I did not step in the 'old firm' might not survive, might not be around to pass to our sons, his and mine. So

I quit politics before the outbreak of World War II and started running the 'old firm' again."

"What happened during the war and during the German occupation?" Henry asked.

Henri Liebaert shrugged, his eyes downcast, he spoke slowly. "It was sad for all of us," he said. "After a while, we were forced by the Nazis to produce textiles for their uniforms. The officer in charge of procurements came to my office. He was delighted to know I spoke German. He assured me that as long as we produced the items they required, the owners and employees would be protected. He handed me a card with a telephone number, a direct line, and said, "If you ever have a problem, just call me."

"Did you ever call him?" my husband asked.

"Of course not!" Liebaert said. "The minute he left, I tore up the card and burned it. Carrying that card would have marked me as a traitor."

Liebaert and his mills were more than lucky because the Nazi régime needed them, indeed. Because of this, they survived the war intact, and after the war ended Liebaert's mills returned to full production, including elastic webbing.

Once Henri Liebaert took us to a pub for lunch where they served typical Belgian food. We ate heaps of wonderful thin French-fried potatoes and hard-boiled eggs accompanied by Belgian beer. He told us that Belgians drink more beer per capita than Germans do. One morning at around six, when we were taking the train to France, we even saw groups of men standing around tables in the station drinking beer for breakfast!

Though an honored dignitary, Henri Liebaert was a very simple man. He would never stand on ceremony or insist on formalities, unless they were required in official affairs or meetings. After a while, he offered to call us by our first names, which was very unusual in Europe. I knew many people who were partners in business, even long time friends, who would still address one another by their last names.

When we visited the Liebaert Mill, in Deinze, Belgium, during the summer of 1961, Henri Liebaert joined us and showed us around. By that time, 48 looms were weaving one-inch elastics exclusively for us, which we sold to manufacturers of men's belts. The noise of those looms was ear shattering. The warps, some in solid colors and some in multicolored patterns or stripes, were rolled on drums and into the looms about thirty-six or forty strips at a time. The little shuttles that brought in the filling yarns seemed to be flying back and forth at terrific speeds; the woven strips came out the front of the loom and were rolled into big cardboard boxes.

These boxes were brought into another room for the finishing process that ensured colorfastness. The process used chemicals that smelled awful but were absolutely essential for colorfast and perspiration proof elastics. It would be a disaster to have colors from a belt come off on white slacks. Next came the packing and shipping. There were already boxes stacked and standing and addressed to HENRY M. YOUNG, INC., NEW YORK.

Henri Liebaert was smiling at me. He said, "Doesn't it feel good to see all these looms working for *Little Margo?*"

On one of our trips to Europe, I went to Brussels by myself while my husband was taking care of business in Italy. Henri Liebaert met me in the lobby of my hotel carrying a big briefcase with business papers. We talked for about an hour. Then he drove me to the Grand Palace in his Oldsmobile 98. This was quite unusual because usually his chauffeur drove the car. "Poor man," Henri said, "why should I take him away from his family in the evening when I am just as happy driving this beautiful car myself?"

The Grand Palace is the jewel of Brussels. At night, the city hall and all the other buildings surrounding the square are illuminated, and it looks like a stage setting for an opera.

We sat together at the window on the second floor of a lovely restaurant facing the glittering city hall. Henri liked good food and he liked to drink Knowing that I liked a Scotch before dinner, he ordered one for each of us, then an appetizer and a wonderful fish dish accompanied by a terrific *Pouilly Fuisse*, one of my favorite white wines.

Henri began telling me stories, about a trip he and his wife had taken to Russia, about other adventures. I was fascinated by his stories.

Suddenly, I realized that someone had put all the chairs upside down on the tables to clean the floors, but obviously nobody dared tell "His Excellency" that they were closing the restaurant and that they might appreciate us getting out of the way. When I pointed this out to Henri, he said, "Oh my, this is quite embarrassing, isn't it?"

Henri Liebaert and his vivacious wife, Jeanne, became very good friends. We were invited to their home in Brussels and their *so-called* cottage in Cap Ferrat. We also met in some other places in Europe, and they would visit us in New York. Due to changing fashion trends, eventually our business with the "old firm" diminished. Still, Henri Liebaert, as the true friend that he had become, would continue to send us handwritten letters in impeccable English. In April of 1972, he wrote:

Henri and Jeanne Liebaert
in Cap Ferrat

"The fact is that things have changed considerably as far as your share of our business is concerned. It is not your fault, nor is it ours that the fashion for men and women has evolved in such a way that men's belts and suspenders cut only a poor figure as compared with days gone by."

In the same letter, he said:

"...but let us not worry, there are so many disagreeable things in the world and in local politics, which certainly are not to your liking either. No use to worry. And for young people like you, it doesn't matter at all. For me, it is good to remember what the French author Mauriac wrote in his *Blue Notes*, 'Politics become of minor importance once you have fallen on your face with the cold breath of eternity."

In another letter dated February 1975, he wrote,

"...I'm glad to notice that my lessons in philosophy have been well understood. I stick to the belief that Philharmony is the love of harmony; Philosophy is the love of wisdom. What more could you want?"

In the last letter we received from him, sometime in December 1976, he said:

"I am not satisfied with the state of the world either and the way things seem to get worse. I feel sorry for the violence at home. There are hold-ups in Brussels almost every day and now there is even the kidnapping of children. I am not satisfied, to put it mildly, with how the 'old firm' is being run. We work three shifts and have a brilliant staff rushing from Munich to London to Paris to Marseilles and Geneva. We are on best terms with our suppliers. However, there are losses because of exchange rates, bad accounts receivable and heavy overhead. I should add that our country has allowed itself the luxury of having the highest wages, social security, and fiscal burdens in the world. But enough said!

If only we had Little Margo in charge of our French market? If only we had Margo working with me? But that is only wishful thinking."

Henri Liebaert died on Easter Sunday, 1977, in Rome. He and his wife had taken their grandchildren to see Rome during their Easter break from school. I miss him, his ideas, and his wonderful letters.

Chapter XXXVII
Daddy's Last Years

My father was very unhappy without my mother. My sister, Vera, offered to buy a larger house so that he could live with her and her family, but he said, "No," and explained to me, "You know, I am too young to be the grandfather in their house. I have to find a new companion. I need to live my life again."

He'd had such a happy marriage and felt he should continue being happy, so he started looking for someone to share his life with. First, there was an old friend in New York, then someone in Canada, but both were not exactly what he was looking for. Then came Jeanne Vellerman, who also lived in Toledo. She had been a widow for a long time, had two married daughters, and made her living in a little dress shop she owned. In fact, my mother and she had been friends. They had met in her dress shop and had discovered they had a lot in common: both were from Europe (Jeanne was born in Holland and her mother was German); they both had two daughters; and both had worked with women's clothes.

After my mother died, Jeanne began pursuing my father. After all, Dad was quite a catch, a nice looking man in his late fifties, immaculately dressed, charming, and well-educated. He earned a good living and, besides, he was lonesome. At the beginning of August 1954, my father and Jeanne Vellerman married. My sister was very upset. A year had not passed since our mother had died, and Jeanne was not particularly pleasant to Vera. She made it quite clear that while she'd married our father, she had no intention of becoming a substitute mother or grandmother. "Don't count on me to baby-sit," she told my sister. "I am not your mother, and your daughters are not my grandchildren." Her own daughters lived out-of-town, and she was glad not to be bothered with motherly or grandmotherly duties for them either. That was Jeanne. But Dad and she got along quite well. She was immaculately clean and a good housekeeper.

They moved into a nice house, traveled, and very much enjoyed their lives together. They made a good match. While Daddy liked to live well and spend money, Jeanne was rather frugal and managed to save for their old age. It was quite a good marriage until Dad got old and sick. Then Jeanne was not as caring and considerate as she should have been, but at least for many years Daddy had a good companion.

Chapter XXXVIII
Around the World Together

Most every year after visiting the various mills that were producing for us, Henry and I took pleasure trips. One year, we cruised the Mediterranean, where we visited the Greek islands and then saw the Acropolis in Athens. We went to Egypt--we started in Alexandria, and we saw Cairo and the Egyptian Museum--by itself worth the trip to Egypt.

Outside of Cairo, we took tours to the pyramids. How small you feel standing next to them, and how phenomenal to see the chambers of the interiors with artifacts from eons ago that you have only read about in books. Cairo at night was a fascinating tableau. From the roof garden of our hotel, we had a panoramic view of the Nile River with all the illuminated boats on its banks.

We went to Israel, the first time anchoring at the Port of Haifa. Like all Jews, I was enraptured to see the land of my fathers and the places I'd read about in the Old Testament and in all our prayer books.

Haifa itself is beautiful, with the sea on one side and the hills behind it. We went to Jerusalem and stood next to the Wailing Wall. Many people were praying, and slips of paper scribbled with requests and messages of thanks were placed between the big blocks in the ancient wall.

Yellow stone walls surrounded the city and all its mosques and churches. New commerce flourished alongside biblical era artifacts in some sections of the city.

Then we went to Tel Aviv, a stark contrast with its modern buildings and coffee houses on the beach; and on to Nazareth and Bethlehem, back again in time, with its many Christian holy places.

Another cruise took us to the Black Sea. Upon entering the Bosporus, we saw before us the many Minarets of Instanbul! We visited the Topkapi Museum and various beautiful mosques, including the magnificent Hagia Sophia! Like Rome, that impressive city is built on seven hills. We spent two beautiful days there.

One of our stops was Odessa, in the Ukraine, where enormous steps, featured in an old film, *Panzerkreuzer Potemkin*, lead up to the entrance of the port. This city is beautiful with wide boulevards and lovely old apartment buildings. It reminded me a great deal of Paris. In the evening, we took a bus to the ornate opera house and saw a magnificent Russian ballet.

When riding through Odessa at night, we could see into many apartments that did not have curtains on the windows. Clotheslines ran back and forth through the rooms. This was a sure sign to me that several families shared one apartment. Despite all the talk, poverty was still predominant in Russia.

Traveling with my Henry was always a pleasurable adventure. We traveled by car through the so-called "Chateau Country" in France and stopped at a number of beautiful old castles. We also traveled by car through Italy. One year, we flew down to Sicily and spent time at the tip of Italy in *Taormina* within sight of the Vulcan "Stromboli." We took a trip to Mount Aetna, which looked to me like the surface of the moon. We were taken by a jeep up high and had to wear special high boots while we walked through the volcano's lava; Mount Aetna was growling.

Even if Henry had never been to a place, he always knew so much about it. He had learned about it in school or read about it or taught himself before we visited. He was always full of get-up-and-go, like I was, and since both of us liked the same things, we always had a great time.

It was good for both of us to temporarily forget about the business and about the details of everyday living. We were there to take in the beauty and to enjoy what we experienced on these wonderful voyages. And we did.

Chapter XXXIX

Celebrating the Holidays Abroad

S ince September is usually the time when our most important Jewish holy days occur--New Year's (*Rosh Hashanah*) and the Day of Atonement (*Yom Kippur*)--I always insisted on attending Jewish services, no matter where Henry and I were when we were traveling.

The Kol Nidre service in *Juan Les Pins*, where we had gone after Paris, was festive, and somewhat strange because the members of this congregation were predominantly from North Africa. Their service was Sephardic rather than Ashkenazi--a variation from the ritual most European Jews follow.

Because of my Jewish school education, I can read Hebrew fluently and understand most of the prayers, but it was still difficult to follow the Sephardic version of the service.

As is the tradition, the cantor and the rabbi carried the Torah through the sanctuary while chanting. The congregation touched the Torah--the men with their talises, and the women with their prayer books--and everyone kissed the Torah and become part of this holy festivity.

Another time, I attended Rosh Hashanah services in the big synagogue in Milan, Italy. These were also *Sephardic* services, which in most instances were Orthodox, meaning that women and men were separated. In this large and beautiful synagogue, as in many, the women sat upstairs in a balcony.

I do not like to attend services without a prayer book, but my Italian was not good enough to ask someone where I might find one. As I was walking up the stairs with a number of other women, I said to the person next to me, "Is there anyone here who speaks English?" The woman next to me answered in a beautiful Southern drawl, "I should say so. I am from Atlanta, Georgia."

I laughed and told her what I wanted, and she immediately spoke to her sister, who was walking with us. When we were seated, the *schammes* (a synagogue assistant) brought us prayer books.

It turned out to be a beautiful service, and during some quiet moments my new "friend" from Atlanta told me that her whole family had been originally from the Greek island of Rhodes. After 35 years of living in the United States, she was visiting all her brothers and sisters who lived in various parts of Europe, as well as seeing those who'd stayed in Rhodes.

On another Yom Kippur, we vacationed in Ascona, in Switzerland. There was a small hotel a block down the street from where we were staying. Our concierge had told us that there would be Yom Kippur services there, so I took a walk down along the beautiful *Lago Maggiore* and spoke to the person in charge. One of their large party rooms was converted for the services. They would not accept any kind of donation from me; all they asked was that we take the meal before the *Kol Nidre* services with them, for which there was a minimal charge. We did. It was terrible food, but we said to ourselves that we were doing a good deed just before the start of our most important holy day.

As an honored guest, Henry was seated in the front row. This embarrassed him because he could not read Hebrew. The ultra-Orthodox service was no hardship for me, but poor Henry was miserable. I had to sit with the other women in the back of the room and we were separated from the men by a curtain.

Henry awoke next morning saying he had a slight fever—that

he didn't feel well—and that he hoped he wasn't going to spoil our trip. This got him off the hook for the services. I didn't challenge him. I didn't even take his temperature, poor dear.

I arranged for his breakfast to be served in the room, gave him some aspirin, brought him the daily newspaper, and went off to attend Yom Kippur services on my own. There, a young woman next to me scolded me for not wearing a head covering, which is the law for all Orthodox married women. When I came back for the afternoon services, after providing lunch for my not-so-sick, hooky-playing husband, I made sure to find a scarf to tie around my head. My "enforcer" smiled, as I was now observant.

Services over, I came back to the hotel, and Henry said, "Can you believe I'm feeling just fine now, no more fever! I guess we can take off tomorrow anyway, no need to lay around for me. I just needed some rest, it seems. I'm all better now."

I understood why.

Chapter XL
Into Africa

One of the best trips we ever took was a safari to Kenya. It was organized by the well-known Swiss travel organization, Kuoni. We flew to Zurich where we met our guide, Dr. C.A.W. Guggisberg, and his wife. He was extremely interesting and had worked first for the British and then for the Kenyan government. After his retirement, he served as a guide a few times a year.

Dr. Guggisberg had a degree in archeology and geology, had authored a number

Dr. Guggisberg's book about Africa

of books, and spoke several languages. He knew every nook and cranny of Kenya and was an expert about its animals, birds, and insects. With his imposing white beard, he made quite a formidable impression. His wife, Rosanne, was also very knowledgeable, but she seemed more the motherly type who wanted to hold her protective arms around us. We were a small group, and Henry and I were the only Americans. In this group, there were a young couple from Belgium, two men from Switzerland, and three Austrians.

Dr. and Mrs. Guggisberg alternated in two Land Rovers as tour guides. Each car had a driver and a local game warden. Driving through the landscape of Kenya is a unique experience. There were wide savannahs, strange-looking trees and bushes, and free-roaming animals, which until then we had only seen in zoos. We were on our way to *Masai Mara*, and our first stop was along a river in a small tent colony.

The main tent was elegant and featured a full bar and a lovely restaurant, where we were served a very good dinner. Afterwards, they escorted us to our individual tents. This night a game warden was accompanied by a hippopotamus that had come up from the river. He did not bother us at all, just marched peacefully with us to our tent. After that, the warden chased him back into the river.

Our tent had two sleeping cots, a few small tables, and two chairs, plus a small room with a shower and toilet with running water. The door and windows were closed with huge zippers. Henry made sure that everything was zipped up before we went to sleep. "I don't want to have a run-in with a hippo or something else during the night," he said. "I'll stick to seeing them in the daytime, in the wild, thank you very much."

We slept beautifully. A young man awakened us at six o'clock and brought us tea, a habit left over from British colonial times.

Breakfast was served outdoors next to the main tent, and we made the acquaintance of several semi-tame animals surrounding our table, including a monkey who jumped up, hoping to join us for breakfast. We loaded suitcases into the Land Rovers and off we went into the African countryside.

It was a serene early morning. The colors were vibrant and incredible. Soon we encountered a huge herd of wildebeests running as if the devil was chasing them. After them came an enchanting herd of elephants, led by a huge female, then followed by elephants of all sizes, including very young ones that walked between the legs of their mothers.

Our guide said, "Only females and their young live in a herd. The males travel separately, usually two or three together." The males are of tremendous size, as we saw on another day when we encountered two of them fighting on their hind legs. When our driver saw them, he stepped on the gas and sped away. Our guide said, "It's great to watch something like that, but when they are angry they can charge and turn this car into matchsticks. It's best to leave them be."

Buffalo on safari in Africa

Every morning, a "boy," as the British called them, woke us with a knock and brought tea. After an early breakfast, we would get into the Land Rovers, ride through ever-changing scenery, and wonder which animals we would see that day. We saw so many but we enjoyed them all: tall giraffes nibbling for food at the top of a tree; lionesses playing with their small cubs; zebras and impalas. There were water buffaloes and ostriches and monkeys of all descriptions. We saw antelopes and gazelles every day.

We always went back to our temporary residence for lunch and then had an hour or two to rest. Henry liked to take a nap, while I swam if there was a pool. In one of the places we visited, our room had louver windows, which we kept open for fresh air. Henry was taking a nap when all of a sudden he woke to a terrible noise. Monkeys had crawled through the windows and were making off with my can of hairspray and whatever other shiny objects they could find, jumping all over the room and screaming at the top of their voices.

I find it hard to describe the atmosphere and the feelings we had while traveling for two weeks through spectacular Kenya. Every day was a magical adventure: seeing all these animals running freely in nature; seeing them eating and mating and feeding their young ones; seeing them serene or hostile; seeing them building and destroying.

We watched the sun rise and the sun set over the vast savannah. We crossed rivers in small boats amid alligators and more hippos. We stopped at lakes with bamboo growing at the edges, where all kinds of birds and water creatures made their homes.

At night, we spied animals going to the rivers and water holes to drink, all of this unique and unforgettable.

Henry, who was an avid photographer, filmed everything, so we could relive this wonderful experience at home. When flying back to Switzerland from Kenya, Henry took a picture of the top of Mount Kilimanjaro, just as the sun was coming up. We had it enlarged and it hangs beautifully framed in our apartment as a lasting memory of this trip.

Henry and I took many fascinating trips together. We went to Mexico and visited parts of Peru, Argentina, and Brazil. We went to London and Paris many times. We took a cruise through the Norwegian Fjords, venturing even further north until we were 500 miles south of the North Pole, completely surrounded by glaciers. For me, looking back, however, I think our Hemingway-esque safari in Kenya remains the absolute highpoint of our travels together.

PART V

Chapter XLI
Henry's Accident

It seems like a lifetime ago that Henry went back to Germany to talk to our manufacturer near *Bayreuth*. He also made a date to meet one of his friends at a Spa at *Lake Constance* (Bodensee). Henry, as usual, rented a car on his arrival in Nuremberg, and after finishing his business discussions began driving to *Lake Constance*. The route goes through Austria, mostly on two-lane mountain roads. Somewhere near Innsbruck, Henry had a terrible accident.

A small sports car, coming from the opposite direction, tried to pass a long line of cars headed by a huge truck and suddenly pulled out and sped straight toward Henry. Henry saw him and immediately swerved his car as far as he could to the right to avoid a head-on collision. By doing so, he almost rolled off the road onto the embankment. He then swung his car back to the left, but the little Opel he was driving at a fairly high rate of speed could not withstand this maneuver and spun out of control rolling over twice and landing on its roof. The sports car that had caused the accident disappeared, and so did all the other cars that were coming from the opposite direction. Fortunately, a German couple, vacationing in Austria, was driving behind Henry, and stopped when they saw what happened. The man tried to pull Henry out of the car, which at this point was on the verge of exploding. Henry was fully conscious and told this complete stranger, "Please, please whatever you do, make sure that you find my passport and my ring." The ring was a gold and lapis lazuli ring I had given him, and somehow it must have slipped off his little finger during the accident. What an incredible presence of mind!

Once the passport and ring were found, Henry was safely pulled out of his car and helped to the side of the road. While the wife waved on-coming cars out of the way, the husband went to the next village for help, but he had a terrible time getting an ambulance. It seems the spot where the accident took place was in some kind of three-county no-man's zone and nobody wanted to take responsibility. But this Good Samaritan was persistent and told the authorities that the accident victim would die if immediate help was not provided. He finally managed to get an ambu-lance that took Henry to the University Hospital in Innsbruck. There, he was admitted to a modern accident treatment pavilion, which had been built for the Winter Olympics a year or two earlier.

The next morning, the telephone operator in our New York of-fice received a call which she could not understand. It was in Ger-man. She called me and said, "There is someone speaking German. Please take over." I thought it was Henry calling me through a German telephone operator, but, instead, a man identifying him-self as Dr. Gasser came to the phone. When I heard the word "doctor," my heart skipped a few beats. Did Henry have a heart at-tack, or might he even be dead? These were the first thoughts that crossed my mind. But Dr. Gasser eased my worries immediately by explaining that he was merely a dentist who had hurt his foot with a lawn mower, and he was in the same hospital room with Henry, who was well enough to talk to me but was unable to make the connection himself. What a relief to hear my beloved's voice saying, "Muckel, I had an automobile accident and some slight in-juries, but I will be fine."

"I will come as soon as I can get a flight over," I replied. And I did.

I called a friend of ours who worked at *Lufthansa* and that same afternoon I was on a flight to Munich, which was the closest air-port to *Innsbruck*. I packed a big suitcase for myself and included clothes, underwear, and shoes for Henry because I had the notion that his suitcase was lost in the accident. Who knew how long I would stay, and, as it turned out, it took many weeks until we got back to New York. I arrived in Munich in the morning but had to wait until 1:00 p.m. to get a train to Innsbruck. I was in no mood to go into Munich, so I spent the hours in the train station restaurant, reading, talking to people, and drinking too many cups of coffee. The train ride from Munich to Innsbruck took me through beautiful scenery, but I really could not enjoy it as I was always thinking of my poor Henry in the hospital. I had advised Dr. Gasser of my arrival, and to my surprise and delight Mrs. Gasser was at the station to help me get to the hotel *Tyrol* where they had made a reservation for me. We had a very difficult time getting my heavy suitcase down the stairs from the railroad platform. As is the case in so many smaller stations in Europe, there was no elevator.

I immediately took a taxi to the hospital, which was modern and pleasant and had big picture windows. My poor Henry was very happy to see me that soon. He had an injury to his hand, and there were still lots of glass splinters and dirt all over his head. The attending nurse told me that they did not want to touch his head for fear of infections. While that seemed a bit strange to me, Henry was in some pain but otherwise well cared for. The head nurse was a Catholic nun who was one of the kindest and most compassionate women I have ever met.

When Dr. Gasser left, they did not put another patient in the second bed, and the head nurse told me that I could nap there anytime I got tired. The evening nurse was a young woman, I believe only eighteen years old, who with the help of only one other person took care of a whole floor of accident patients. She also provided me with snacks, fried eggs, coffee, and a variety of other goodies, so I could keep Henry company instead of going out for lunch or dinner. His hand did not heal well at all, and he also complained of pain in his shoulder, which they treated with heat lamps. Later on in New York, it was diagnosed that his shoulder was dislocated. It could have been remedied right there, but the doctors in *Innsbruck* did not recognize the problem. Later on, it would have required a very difficult operation to remedy the problem, so Henry decided against it and lived the rest of his life unable to move his arm completely. We spent three weeks in *Innsbruck*, and while poor Henry was confined to the hospital I walked through *Innsbruck* every day on my way from my hotel. Innsbruck is a beautiful, old city surrounded by mountains, some of them snow-capped. I walked through inspiring streets each day, finding interesting architecture and landscaping and charming little inns and restaurants, knowing I was lucky to have my Henry alive.

After three weeks, Henry could leave the hospital, but he was instructed to come back two to three weeks later so that doctors could re-examine the healing of his hand. We went to a delightful resort in the Austrian Alps. Although it was toward the end of June, the weather was miserable and we could hardly venture outdoors. Our friend Max Hausman, who lived in *Milano* at that time, told us, "Come to the *Eden Hotel*, in *Lugano*, Switzerland, where the weather is warm and sunny, and I will meet you there." We took the train through the mountains and along the lakes of Austria, and a short time later arrived at the *Eden Hotel*. The room was furnished with white leather club chairs and looked directly out on the lake. Max met us and we spent a lovely ten days there relaxing, walking, and enjoying good restaurants. There were no noticeable after-effects from the accident. Henry walked as well as ever. The difficulties only appeared much, much later. However, Henry's hand had not yet healed, and we had to make the long, tedious, train ride back to *Innsbruck*.

While we were still at the hospital, Henry received a post card from the nice couple who had, for all intents and purposes, saved his life after the accident. It was addressed to the "Unknown American Patient at *Innsbruck University Hospital*" and read as follows, "We are the people who helped you after the accident. Please let us know how you are doing. We hope you have fully recovered and would love to hear from you." It was signed Fritz und Maggi Urtnowski. I called them up and thanked them for their wonderful help and told them that Henry was recovering nicely. When we got back home, we sent them a beautiful silver bowl and later invited them to come and visit us in New York.

Fritz Urtnowski was hesitant to go on such a long trip and fly over the Atlantic Ocean. He'd never traveled further than the mountains of Germany, Austria, or Switzerland, but his wife, son, and daughter-in-law talked him into it. All four of them came to New York the next year. Neither Fritz nor Maggi spoke a word of English. Their son, Guenter, spoke a little bit, but their daughter-in-law, Len, a beautiful, charming Dutch woman, spoke it fluently. She worked for an American company in *Düsseldorf.* We had a wonderful time with all of them. We showed them New York by car and went sightseeing by boat. We also took them to the Barnum & Bailey Circus. "You couldn't have given Fritz a greater pleasure," Maggi told us, and sure enough Fritz laughed

Fritz and Maggi Urtnowski

Guenter and Len Urtnowski

and smiled throughout the entire show. They came back a few years later, and we also visited them at their home. Once they surprised us on a Rhine River boat cruise. We became really good friends and wrote to each other very often. Maggi died a few yeas ago, but Fritz, who is now in his eighties, is alive and quite well. Last year, Guenter and Len came to Florida just to visit me. I thought this was a wonderful token of the friendship we had developed. After all, it is not every day that someone saves your life; nor does the chance often come again to act honorably.

My beloved Henry, who was always so active and who always walked so fast that I could hardly keep up with him, gradually developed difficulties walking. Examinations showed that he needed a hip replacement. It was a complicated procedure at that time – three weeks in a hospital bed with a device between his legs to make sure that the hip would heal properly. After that, therapy and a nurse at home, but he recovered nicely and resumed his usual activities at the office and at home. We traveled again and enjoyed our lives. But then, about a year later, he started complaining again that walking was becoming more and more difficult. He thought that he might have to have another hip replaced. But the surgeon who had performed the first hip replacement examined him and said, "It is not your hip, it is your back. I know a great surgeon specializing in back operations. Please go see him."

After an MRI, Henry was diagnosed with stenosis of the spine. The doctor, a South African, assured Henry and me that the operation would restore his normal walking in a short period of time. "I just had a patient your age who had the same operation," he added. "He now walks all the way from the Westside through Central Park to see me at my office" (which was at 88th and 5th Avenue). Henry was a great believer that an operation, if done well, would help. So he agreed.

Indeed, at first the operation seemed to be successful. After a period of recuperation, Henry could walk rather well and was so happy to be his old self again. However, the pleasure was short-lived. After a few months, walking difficulties reappeared and his condition deteriorated severely. Even a walk from our garage to the office, which covered a distance of only two blocks, became difficult. A consultation with the surgeon and further examinations showed that adhesions had developed. "O.K.," said the doctor, "We will operate again and we'll remove the adhesions."

However, by now, Henry was no longer convinced that an operation was a "cure all," and he refused to consent to another one. But while he certainly was unhappy about his fate, he would not give up the lifestyle we had established. We went to restaurants, concerts, theaters, operas, and, of course, we saw our friends. We even went on various trips overseas and took our new companion, a wheel chair, along. I was strong, and I could push it even on the cobblestones of Paris. Fortunately, Henry could still walk in the apartment and to his seat in a theater and into a restaurant, in other words, short distances. So we still had a good life in spite of his handicap.

Our last trip overseas was on the QE II in October 1990, when we visited Henry's cousins in England and from there flew to Berlin. Henry enjoyed being back in his hometown, and I enjoyed it with him. We had a wonderful driver who took us wherever we wanted to go, including the Weissensee Cemetery where Henry's grandfather is buried. He had died young of a kidney disease and Henry had adored him. His beloved grandmother is buried in Jerusalem, where she went to live during the Hitler years to live with her son and daughter-in-law, Henry's Uncle George and Aunt Alice. From Berlin, we flew back to London and across the Atlantic on the *Concorde* to New York. It was an unforgettable experience crossing the ocean in a little bit over three hours. I used to tell people, "By the time they served us a cognac after dinner, we were already back home in New York."

Chapter XLII
Henry's Funeral

My husband Henry's death--on October 10, 1993-- closed a large chapter of my life. Henry, of course, until the day he died, *was* my life. He had been my lover, my best friend, and my business partner. We had looked forward to a long, leisurely retirement in Florida, and now he was gone. I was devastated.

The whole family came to his funeral: My sister, Vera, and her husband, Louis; my nieces, Linda and Nancy with their husbands from Toledo, Ohio. Henry's sister, Jill, and her daughter, Terry, came from California, and my cousin, Walter, and his wife, Lonnie, came from Butler, Pennsylvania, where Walter was leading a congregation as rabbi and cantor.

I wanted my cousin, Walter, to conduct the funeral. It is so much more personal to have a close relative do it, instead of a strange rabbi. The night before the funeral, Walter assembled the whole family in my living room and asked each family member to tell him what they remembered best about Henry. It was so heart-warming to hear how much he was loved and admired by everyone. Henry had always said that he wanted his funeral to be a celebration of his life; in fact, he wanted music there. He requested that his favorite piece, the Intermezzo from *Cavalleria Rusticana*, be played, as well as a *Largo* from Handel because it had been played at his grandfather's funeral. Despite all my grief, I was able to find the proper tapes, and Walter played them at the funeral. Our nephew, Stanley, wrote a heart-warming eulogy about his Uncle Henry, and Terry read it. George Stein, a friend and lodge brother, spoke beautifully and so did Walter, of course, who incorporated all the wonderful things our family had told him about Henry with his own reflections and recollections. But before Walter spoke, he turned to the wall behind Henry's casket where the *23rd Psalm* had been imbedded. Knowing that Henry always hated this psalm, he knocked on the casket and said, "Sorry, Henry, but this we could not help."

Henry, dear Henry, would have wanted a celebration of life and not a sad funeral, and we did, indeed, provide that for him. My contribution was a passage from the book, *September*, by Rosamunde Pilcher, which reads as follows.

"Death is nothing at all. It does not count. I have only slipped away into the next room. Nothing has happened. Everything remains exactly as it was. I am I, and you are you, and the old life that we lived so fondly together is untouched, unchanged. Whatever we were to each other, that we are still. Call me by the old familiar name. Speak of me in the easy way which you always used. Put no differences into your tone. Wear no forced air of solemnity or sorrow. Laugh as we always laughed at the little jokes that we enjoyed together. Play, smile, think of me, pray for me. Let my name be ever the household word that it always was. Let it be spoken without an effort, without the ghost of a shadow upon it. Life means all that it ever meant. It is the same as it ever was. There is absolute and unbroken continuity. What is this death but a negligible accident? Why should I be out of mind, because I am out of sight? I am but waiting for you, for an interval, somewhere very near, just round the corner. All is well."

Then we all went to my apartment for sandwiches and drinks and I lifted my glass and said, "Henry, this is your last party, my love." My cousin, Walter, wrote in his yearly letter to the family:

"My Cousin Margo's husband died in Bal Harbour, Florida in October. He was 83 and had been ill for some time. His death, though quicker than anticipated, was not totally unexpected. He had been a person who had enjoyed and lived life to the fullest. Margo made sure that his funeral service, which I conducted, was not morbid, but a celebration of his life. For four days, Margo took his friends and family to all the restaurants he'd savored the most. Their beachfront apartment became a gathering place, and we enjoyed the beach, the pool, the food, and the company. Even though we talked a lot about Henry, we also felt quite guilty for having such a good time. But Margo kept reassuring us that this is exactly what Henry would have wanted. Not every death lends itself to such commemoration, but it is certainly something to be considered. When I die, I hope that people will come together joyfully to sing all the songs that I used to sing with them when I was alive."

Henry is buried in the Menorah Cemetery on Griffin Road, in Fort Lauderdale. I selected a location that faces a little pond. I thought to myself how we both loved to look out on the water. Then I said, "Stupid, isn't it? When we are in the mausoleum, we won't be able to see the view." Never mind, it doesn't matter. When I go to the cemetery, either on the anniversary of his death or on his birthday, the beautiful surroundings soothe me. But after all these years I still miss my beloved Henry, and not a day goes by when I do not think about him.

The Henry Young Mausoleum

Chapter XLIII
The Widow

After Henry's funeral, after everybody left, after forty-four years of a wonderful marriage to a man I had known and loved for more than two-thirds of my life, I found myself all alone. It was a strange feeling. Could I continue by myself, and what were my choices? I briefly considered suicide, but I discarded the idea quickly. I felt that there were still too many things I wanted to do, to see, and to accomplish. And there was one thing I did not want to be and that was a weeping widow. I didn't want my friends to feel sorry for me. I was not going to wait for their phone calls and invitations. No, I was going to show them that my life alone was going to continue in the same way it did when Henry was alive.

Five weeks after the funeral, I gave a dinner party in my house for all of my close friends. I would show them: Life was going to continue, even without Henry. Yes, it was tough, and yes, I felt lonely and sorry for myself, and yes, I did shed some tears. But I told myself, "Life must go on." I joined a bridge club. I continued to invite my friends to parties in my house. I visited my friends in New York and my family in Toledo, Ohio.

But still, I was restless. And I knew that even though I am usually a very positive person, depression might lurk right around the corner. If I stayed in one place--if I fell into a routine at home--I knew loneliness would come knocking. But I also knew it was

353

hard for anyone or anything to hit a moving target. So I decided to travel. I'd hit the road again. I might be too old for vagabonding--and too set in my ways for roughing it--but I could and I would travel. I'd spent my entire life on the move, and my positive attitude and my exuberance for adventure were always what saved me. I would do it again. Look out world, here I come (*again*).

I asked my sister, Vera, and her husband, Louis, to join me and we had wonderful times together. Our first trip started in London, where I introduced them to Henry's cousins and their families who had adopted me as part of their family. Then Charles, the husband of an old school friend of Vera's, picked us up from our hotel and took us to their home where, in their beautiful garden surrounded by flowers, we enjoyed a wonderful dinner prepared by Vera's friend, Lotte. We also took the train to *Feltham*, in *Middlesex*, and visited the son of the woman Vera grew up with when she first came to England. His wife, two children, and his parents joined us. Vera reminisced with Margaret about the time they lived together. We all had a great day.

Looking back, I am sure I traveled so much to keep the loneliness from taking root and to remind myself I was alive. I kept a step ahead of any depression and I succeeded. What's more, I enjoyed myself tremendously and I began to appreciate even more the years I lived with Henry and the memories those years provide. On another occasion, Vera, Louis, and I flew to Spain and took a cruise out of Barcelona along the Spanish and French coasts. I had so much fun showing them the places where I had been with Henry, like *Nice* and *Monte Carlo*. I could relive my memories and at the same time serve as tour guide. But I could also experience things I hadn't experienced before. We stopped in Florence, where I had never been. Then, from *Livorno*, Vera and I took a train to *Pisa* to see the *Leaning Tower*. I was strengthening my bonds to Vera and Louis, and I continued to hear my mother's admonition

"Take care of your little sister, Vera." Our last stop was *Civitavec-chia*; from there, we took a taxi into Rome. Louis had been there on a furlough from the Army and had always wanted to show Vera this magnificent, interesting, and historical city.

We went on cruises and again I was delighted to show them the places I had been with Henry. We went to Spain, France, and Italy. In July 1998, we flew back to Hamburg and celebrated Vera's seventy-third birthday at the *Vier Jahreszeiten Hotel*, which is still the best hotel in Hamburg. I remember saying to my sister, "Isn't it nice to once again celebrate your birthday in the city where you were born?" And it was. From there, we flew to Stockholm and took a cruise on the *Baltic Sea* and visited *Saint Petersburg* and the many other interesting ports.

But *Saint Petersburg* was, indeed, the outstanding highlight: its architecture, its bridges, and, most of all, the *Hermitage* museum. Too bad we could only spend two and one-half hours there! The other ports included *Helsinki, Finland; Tallinn, Estonia;* and *Vasby, Sweden.* The wonderful guides brought each new city to life. The last stop of the cruise was *Copenhagen*, where I had been before with my dear Henry. I particularly enjoyed showing Vera and Louis the exquisite *Tivoli Gardens.*

Another time, we took a cruise on the *Danube*, and we stopped in *Budapest* for two days. Then we went into Vienna. Vera thought we would hear *Vienna Waltzes* everywhere we went; well, we almost did but not quite. One afternoon, I took them to a garden restaurant where they played all of our favorite Viennese melodies while we enjoyed *Jause* (coffee and cake). We went to the *Volksoper* where we watched a delightful performance of *The Fledermaus.* Only the Viennese can perform a Viennese Operetta that well. We also saw *Schloss Schoenbrunn.* I filmed the entire interior of the castle, including its vast collection of art, as well as the beautiful gardens. On another evening, we went to a concert in an old castle.

We enjoyed Vienna tremendously. From there, a driver took us to Prague, which remains one of the most beautiful and interesting cities that I have ever seen.

We used every excuse we could find and took advantage of every opportunity to travel. For Vera's and Louis' golden wedding anniversary, we flew to L.A. and took a cruise on the beautiful *Vistafjord* through the Panama Canal. We first stopped in Acapulco, now more developed than the time I was there with Henry, but still as beautiful. We then stopped in Puerto Caldera, Costa Rica. At the pier, we found a guide--a friendly, roly-poly gentleman--who knew a driver with a small, old car. All four of us piled into it. Louis sat in front with the driver and Vera and I sat in the back, the guide in-between us. It was a terribly hot day and the old car had no air conditioning, so I said to Vera when we stopped, "That fellow squeezed against us from either side would be good on a cold winter day." But he was a jovial young man and a very good guide.

We stopped on a hilly roadside where he let us pick coffee beans from the bushes; when the old car stalled, we thought we would be stranded up there for a long time. But the driver got the car going again, and after an outdoor lunch and a ride though the lush countryside, we entered San Jose, the vibrant capital of Costa Rica. San Jose is a charming city with an old opera house, built by the same architect who designed the Paris *Opera House*. We were fortunate enough to visit the inside furnished in the old style, and our guide once again gave us a wonderful tour. As it turned out, he was very knowledgeable about opera houses in Europe and around the world.

During the trip through the Panama Canal, I spent most of the day on the balcony of my cabin photographing the locks and the surrounding countryside. I was fascinated by how a small railroad locomotive pulled our huge ship through the narrow canal. We then found ourselves in the Caribbean, and after a few stops at various islands, we landed back in Fort Lauderdale.

For Vera's seventy-fifth birthday, I took the whole family to Las Vegas: Vera and Louis; their daughters, Linda and Nancy; and their respective husbands. We all stayed at the Bellagio for four days. We fell in love with the hotel and enjoyed all that was offered to us: luxurious rooms, elegant bars and restaurants, a gallery of fine art, three swimming pools set in landscaped surroundings, and a magnificent casino. We hired a limousine to take us through the new housing developments and the impressive countryside. We visited a number of the other hotels, saw lovely shows, and enjoyed a special birthday dinner at the exquisite French restaurant, *Le Cirque*.

Vera and her daughters at Vera's seventy-fifth birthday party

For New Year's 2000, we took a *Millennium* cruise out of Buenos Aires to celebrate the new century in the Bay of Rio de Janeiro. It was my second visit to Buenos Aires but the first time Vera and Louis had been there. All three of us enjoyed this beautiful city with its wide boulevards and many parks and tango shows. It feels like a mixture of both Paris and Madrid.

We were lucky because the jeweler, *Stern*, whose headquarters are in Rio, provided us with a car, a driver, and a guide. Rio bustled more than ever just before New Year's Eve. We couldn't even get to Copacabana Beach, but we were able to spend some time in the vast *Botanical Gardens* and despite Vera's initial objections we managed a trip by cable car to the top of the *Sugarloaf*; she is not comfortable with heights or with cable cars. In the end, we enjoyed the ride and the view from the top was well worth it.

We continued along the Brazilian coast, with stops at Recife and Belém, and we then crossed the equator and sailed into the Caribbean, stopping in Trinidad, Grenada, St. Lucia, Barbados, and, of course, finally back home in Fort Lauderdale. As always, we had a great time.

Vera and Louis have been wonderful to me. They are terrific to be with--we always understand one another so well--and we always have a good time together. Some years back, they moved into a beautiful condo on Sunny Isles Beach, just one mile away from me. For the last few years, they've spent six months during the winter here in Florida, and I am extremely happy that we are able to dedicate as much time as possible to one another.

They are not only my closest family, but they are also my dearest friends. Vera is still my "little" sister, and Louis is like the "big brother" I never had. They enhance my life, especially when they are with me in Florida.

But I have traveled by myself, too. Once or twice a year, I visit New York, which I still love dearly and consider my hometown. After all, I lived there most of my life. I enjoy the hustle and bustle of this fascinating city, the wonderful concerts and theater, and, of course, all my friends who are still there. I have been to California and Oregon to visit friends and family, and two years ago a dear friend and I flew to Milan, Italy, and then to Venice, to take a cruise through the Greek Islands. It was an incredible experience. On my birthday, August 24th, we stopped in Athens, where the temperature was 104 degrees, and climbed all the way up to the Acropolis. Even though we are not young anymore, my friends and I can (and do) enjoy life. The evening culminated in an elaborate celebration dinner at a charming rooftop restaurant.

I am all alone now--or should I say I live alone--but I continue living life to the fullest, and I have learned how to move forward without forgetting the past.

Chapter XLIV
The Balmoral

I did something very daring. In the summer of 2000, I bought myself a beautiful condominium. Why would I want to do that? Well, all kinds of reasons. I wanted more room. A single person living alone really doesn't need that much room, but it can be wonderful to have it. Crazy? Perhaps. I wanted an office, since I spend so much time at my desk and computer. A den or bedroom is always messed up by working there, but a *room of one's own* would be heaven. I wanted a den large enough to have a permanent card table. I play a lot of bridge now, and what a pain it is to drag a bridge table and four chairs out of a closet. So I found this gorgeous, two bedroom apartment with three bathrooms, a wrap around terrace, a large kitchen with windows and breakfast nook, and with all rooms facing the ocean on the 10th floor of the Balmoral, in Bal Harbour.

I hired a decorator, wall-papered every room, and replaced every appliance, every light fixture, and every doorknob. I also built a glass wall to create my office, a room surrounded by windows, all of which look out on the ocean. Somehow, the view changes and seems different every day. In spite of the beautiful view--perhaps because of it--I accomplish all my work accompanied by a breeze from the ocean and classical music from my radio.

And what work is it that I am doing? First of all, I have been writing this book, my memoirs. And now the computer sitting next to my desk has also become my companion. I take care of my investments and keep detailed records of all of them. There is homework from my Spanish class (I thought it would be practical to learn Spanish since I live in the Miami area where a majority of people speak Spanish). There is the daily mail, bills to be paid, and letters to be written. In the end, my office has become the place where I spend most of my time.

The living and dining room combination is great for entertaining. And I love to give dinner parties. Drinks and hors d'hoeuvres are served in my living room; then dinner is served around my dining table, which is set with my Rosenthal dishes and crystal glasses. Eight people can sit comfortably, but I

The dining table set for company at the Balmoral, Bal Harbour, Florida

can also accommodate ten, and if there are more I can add an extra table and manage 15, which is important during the holidays.

My den was the master bedroom, where I now have a Murphy bed for guests, a built-in television, and a recliner from which I occasionally watch television. In a corner, there is an attractive, made-to-order glass table for playing cards. I also bought four beautifully upholstered chairs, so much more comfortable than regular bridge chairs.

Where do I sleep? In the second bedroom. I bought a new bedroom set of shiny, eggshell-colored Formica with gold-colored metal inserts. When I wake up in the morning, I see the ocean through the window. I seldom close the curtains, so as not to miss the beautiful view.

Right below me is the swimming pool (which I love) and my cabana. The cabana has a small terrace behind it that is covered by palm trees; it faces the ocean and is very peaceful. There I com-

Margo in front of the Balmoral,
Bal Harbour, Florida

pose my ideas for writing. The cabana is furnished with a table, chairs, a cabinet, and a refrigerator; it also has a glass enclosed shower. It is my second home, where I give lively parties on the Fourth of July. From the roof of the cabana, we can watch the fireworks on the beach, our attention turned toward the sudden bursts of light that illuminate for brief moments the vast darkness of the universe.

Chapter XLV

Harbour House

How sad to see three huge heaps of rubble where an impressive 20-story apartment building once stood. For almost eight years, we called The Harbour House our winter home. The destruction did not happen all at once. But on October 1, 2003, the remaining tenants vacated their apartments. Each time I crossed the Haulover Bridge from Sunny Isles Beach, the building looked at me with its sad abandoned eyes, and each time the deterioration became worse. First, there were no more shades on the windows; then, the windows were broken. A little later, frames were gone, and so it went until on January 18, 2004, the building was detonated. It sounded like a bolt of thunder, and the dust covered the people and cars watching the spectacle from Haulover Beach across the inlet.

Harbour House South is still standing and looks rather forlorn without its twin, now just three heaps of rubble to be carried away at some later date to make way for some newer condominiums and a hotel. It will in all likelihood be beautiful, but it does not diminish my sadness.

Henry and I first saw the Harbour House at the occasion of Max Hausman's wedding to Claire Loew on January 30, 1981. Henry was best man; he was one of Max's oldest friends. It was a small, intimate wedding with family and a few friends in the party room of Harbour House South. We liked the location and when we heard that the North Building was renting furnished apartments on a daily and weekly basis, we thought how wonderful it would be instead of renting a hotel for a Florida vacation.

Three years later, in January 1984, we closed our business. Henry felt it was time to retire and enjoy the fruits of our labor. We did not want to spend the cold winters in New York, and we wanted to establish a winter home in Florida. What better place to try this than the furnished apartments in The Harbour House?

In March of 1984, we flew down to Miami, rented a car, and moved into a nice one-bedroom apartment on the main floor of Harbour House North. We arrived on one of the coldest days Miami Beach had seen in years. I can still see my poor Henry taking a walk around the pool dressed in his rain coat with wool lining, the collar pulled up high, a wool scarf around his neck, a cap on his head, and wearing his favorite pig skin gloves which I had hand sewn for him some years earlier. "So this is Florida weather?" he mumbled under his breath as he walked around the pool. Poor guy, the next day he had laryngitis.

I saw a sign in the lobby of the building with the names of three doctors and made an appointment. Dr. Paul Rozynes could see him that afternoon and with proper medication cured him in a few days. That not only saved our vacation but also introduced us to one of the finest, most dedicated doctors and someone who took care of us for many years, until long after Henry's death when he decided to quit private practice.

That was our first experience with Harbour House North. Before making a final decision about where to spend the winter months, we stayed in Palm Beach the next year, but we really did not like it very much. We had no friends there, and it was very difficult to get to know anyone unless you were a permanent resident. Then one day, a friend who lived in Miami Beach called us in New York and said he found out that Harbour House North was now renting seasonal furnished apartments. I called up the renting office, made a date to see them, and flew down for a day to convince myself that it would be nice. And it was. The apartment available on the 11th floor had a terrace (the only strand of apartments in Harbour House North that featured terraces). It was very clean, very bright, and faced south and west. The pleasant lady in the renting office showed me the furniture I could select: all new, modern upholstered chairs and couches for the living room and light wood sets for our two bedrooms. I immediately signed a lease for three months--January, February, March--and went home.

Funny, I thought I would never like being in Florida for more than two weeks, but Harbour House was so beautiful and well kept; the beach--which I love--was in front of the door; there was a great swimming pool; and we had some friends who were also wintering here. We went to the theater, concerts, and the opera. We found nice restaurants and we especially enjoyed the Friday night dinners at The Harbour House restaurant, which was excellent at that time and so well attended that reservations were needed days ahead of time. Unfortunately, the restaurant deteriorated from year to year. It was a real shame.

We did not sign up for the next season, and Henry kept on nudging me, "You better call up and see that we get the 1105 apartment again." But when I called--as early as May--they told me that 1105 was taken but they could give us the same apartment on the 6th floor, 605. They were not giving seasonal rentals again, however, but offered us a yearly contract that was only nominally higher than what we had paid for the three months. It sounded like a good deal and we grabbed it. They also offered a three-year lease with small increases every year. From a three-month stay, we became half-year residents of Miami Beach. We really enjoyed living at Harbour House North from 1986 until 1993. It was, in the truest sense, our second home where we were happy, where we entertained and gave parties, and where we enjoyed the Florida winters. Now Harbour House North is gone forever, but still I am left with some sense of satisfaction. After all, the demolition of a building may destroy the floors and walls that housed the people who lived there, but nothing can ever take away the lives that people lived and the wonderful memories they shared.

Epilogue

My Next Adventure

My next adventure is beginning. I am sitting in a Delta Song plane in Miami, Florida on my way to JFK, in New York. Even the crying baby across the aisle cannot dim my expectations for what I believe will be an exciting journey. The plane begins its slow approach to the runway. It is 6:00 p.m. The sun, still shining, illuminates the other planes parked at their gates, great silver birds ready to take their passengers on who knows what voyage or adventure? The plane I am sitting in is new, and the staff is more polite than I could have hoped for. All in all, I am in a good mood. I am excited to make this exotic journey.

But this is also going to be a sentimental journey. I've never been to the Orient despite the fact that my husband, Henry, and I had successful business connections in Japan and in Hong Kong. Years ago (perhaps it is different now?), women were not accepted in the Oriental business world, and I would have been very much in the way. But Henry had always promised me that once we were retired we would make a trip to the Orient together. He would, he promised, show me all the places he had visited--and perhaps even more. Unfortunately, by the time we stopped working, Henry's health had deteriorated and a trip of that magnitude would have been too strenuous for him. So ten years after his death, I've decided that I must see that part of the world before I, too, become too old to travel.

It is going to be a long flight. It is now 7:00 p.m., our time, and 9:00 a.m. in Japan, the next day. We will arrive at 2:30 p.m. But I am beginning to lose track of time and I don't really care. I have come to understand that time moves in many ways, that time itself is sometimes an illusion and, sometimes, surprisingly unpredictable.

We arrive at Tokyo's International Airport on time at 2:30 p.m. I am dead tired when I check into the *Imperial Hotel*, one of the oldest and finest hotels in Tokyo, where Henry had stayed. I had been traveling since 11:00 a.m., and I had lost a day crossing the date line. I feel like a time traveler in three dimensions. I am here now, re-living the past. And I am very much anticipating the future.

The next day on a tour, we drive through the neighborhoods of Tokyo and then past the Asaka Guest House, a former palace, which is now reserved for visiting dignitaries. We pass the *Imperial Palace and Gardens*. We then stop at the *Asakusa Kannon Temple*, the oldest Buddhist temple in Tokyo. The street leading to it is filled with colorful souvenir shops on both sides, and it reminds me of our Florida flea markets. But the timeless temple itself is quite beautiful.

The last stop is the famous GINZA, the main thoroughfare for shopping and restaurants. How often had Henry mentioned this name, GINZA, and here I am standing on this same street so many years later. All day long driving through this pulsing city, my thoughts were with Henry. When was the last time he was here? Since then, the city must have changed tremendously. Parts of the heavy, old walls were still standing and so were some of the original gates. But Tokyo is now an energetic, modern city with a busy highway running through it. At the same time, it is also an immaculately clean city, as if the streets were washed continuously and yesterday no longer mattered.

In the evening, I take a taxi to the *HAMAMAT-SUCHO* Bus Terminal, and it seems to me that I am arriving at exactly the same spot I started out from when I began my tour that morning. After dinner in a typical Japanese restaurant not far from the terminal, I am driven to a fairly new section of Tokyo called *ROPPONGI HILLS*. It is an "in" place with expensive condos and designer shops, but it still includes an older section filled with small boutiques. I visit the 55th and 56th floors of a sightseer's paradise, a circular 58-story building with floor-to-ceiling windows all around and benches to sit on and enjoy the view of Tokyo at night, lit up in spectacular colors. The landmark of Tokyo, the Tokyo Tower, shines orange in the night sky like a huge matchstick. Tokyo is colorful during the day and the stores are attractively decorated, but at night everything sparkles and glitters and comes alive with the energy of promise: the streets and the windows of the tall buildings are dazzling, and the signs of restaurants and shops-- some featuring oversized, oblong glass containers with the shop's name in Japanese and in English hanging over the door or window--are illuminated.

From the tower, I see how densely populated the city is. There are 12 million people in Tokyo. A few floors further down is a museum of modern art: no paintings but rooms filled with huge red balloons with white polka dots. The balloons are shaped in a variety of forms and they seem infinitely multiplied by the mirrored walls around them. The myriad rooms, the vibrant lighting, the cacophony of noise and sound effects, and the mystical marble sculptures remind me that many of life's voyages are also both inspiring and dizzying.

My trip to the Orient lasted three weeks; my life story covers a good part of the twentieth century and it continues every day.

I have lived a long and varied life. From my youth in Hitler Germany to my retirement in Florida, my life has been filled with adventures, with work, with love, with accomplishments and disappointments, and with energy and a zest for living. I am still looking forward to many more good years surrounded by family and friends, more adventures and more travels as I continue my *voyage through time*.

Manufactured By: RR Donnelley
                     Momence, IL USA
                     July , 2010